D1339586

WINDOWS

ON·THE·WORLD

CARS
and HOW THEY WORK

Written by
Gordon Cruickshank

Illustrated by
Alan Austin

DORLING KINDERSLEY • LONDON

A Dorling Kindersley Book

Editors Marie Greenwood
Stephen Setford
Art editor Christopher Gillingwater
Designer Peter Radcliffe

Senior art editor Chris Scollen

Managing art editor Jacquie Gulliver
Managing editor Ann Kramer

Editorial consultant Christopher Gill
Production Shelagh Gibson

First published in Great Britain in 1992
by Dorling Kindersley Limited,
9 Henrietta Street, London WC2E 8PS

A CIP catalogue record for this book is available
from the British Library.

ISBN 0-86318-939-3

Colour Separations by DOT Gradations Limited
Printed in Spain by Artes Graficas; Toledo S. A.
D.L.TO:963–1992

CONTENTS

STARTING OFF

The motor car is a central part of our lives which we take for granted. It is the result of years of development and improvement. It still works on the same principles as 50 years ago, but uses half the fuel. Today, motorists expect their cars to start instantly and cope with summer heat and winter snows. Rigorous testing on the road and in the laboratory ensures that the modern car is able to withstand all kinds of weather. Electronic engine controls allow it to cruise quietly for hours at more than 110kph (70mph). Thanks to computer design (page 7) it is both lighter and stronger. Every new car undergoes tough safety tests and has seat-belts and safety glass fitted (pages 28-29).

The modern car takes us from place to place faster and more efficiently than ever before. But there has been a price to pay. The increasing number of cars on the road has led to problems with pollution and congestion (pages 58-61). To solve these problems, experts are rethinking the way cars are built, run and used.

Slowing down

Efficient brakes are a crucial part of car safety. The handbrake is operated mechanically by a lever and is usually used when the car is parked. The foot brake slows the car while it is on the move. There are two types of brake: drum and disc. Both work by means of liquid pressure, or hydraulics. When the brake pedal is pressed, it operates a "master" cylinder which pushes the fluid through pipes to small "slave cylinders" on each of the four wheels. The fluid pushes against pistons in the cylinders and the brakes are applied.

In a disc brake, small pads grip both sides of an iron disc attached to the wheel

In a drum brake, shoes press against a metal drum attached to the wheel

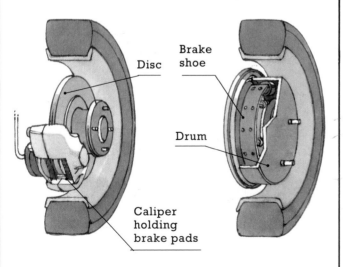

Disc

Brake shoe

Drum

Caliper holding brake pads

Ready to go
Japan's Nissan Sunny is a truly versatile all-rounder. Its powerful engine would once have been at home in a sports car. It has an aerodynamic body (pages 32-33) and front-wheel drive (page 5). Yet with its hatchback and folding seats it can carry large objects with ease.

Before a journey, a good driver checks the oil, water and tyres, and cleans the windows

Windscreen wipers clear the screen in rain or snow; an electric motor drives one and the other is connected to it by a rod or cable

Clear and bright
These headlamps are called sealed-beam units. Each forms one large, especially-bright bulb. Computer design makes sure that the headlamps throw a strong beam without dazzling other drivers (page 45).

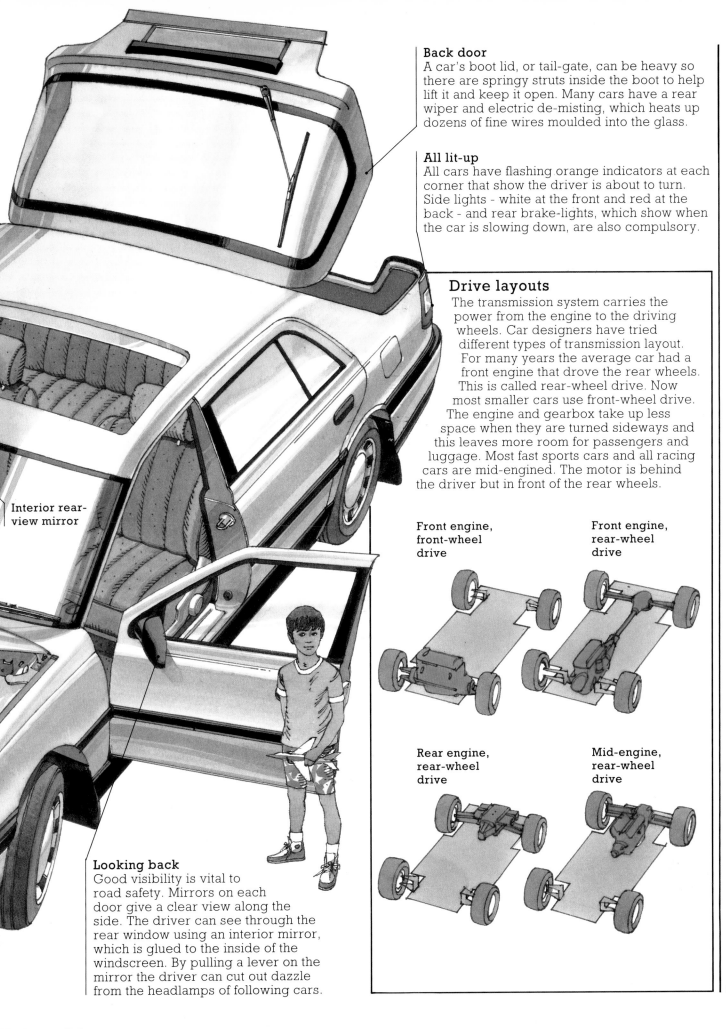

Back door

A car's boot lid, or tail-gate, can be heavy so there are springy struts inside the boot to help lift it and keep it open. Many cars have a rear wiper and electric de-misting, which heats up dozens of fine wires moulded into the glass.

All lit-up

All cars have flashing orange indicators at each corner that show the driver is about to turn. Side lights - white at the front and red at the back - and rear brake-lights, which show when the car is slowing down, are also compulsory.

Drive layouts

The transmission system carries the power from the engine to the driving wheels. Car designers have tried different types of transmission layout. For many years the average car had a front engine that drove the rear wheels. This is called rear-wheel drive. Now most smaller cars use front-wheel drive. The engine and gearbox take up less space when they are turned sideways and this leaves more room for passengers and luggage. Most fast sports cars and all racing cars are mid-engined. The motor is behind the driver but in front of the rear wheels.

Front engine, front-wheel drive

Front engine, rear-wheel drive

Rear engine, rear-wheel drive

Mid-engine, rear-wheel drive

Interior rear-view mirror

Looking back

Good visibility is vital to road safety. Mirrors on each door give a clear view along the side. The driver can see through the rear window using an interior mirror, which is glued to the inside of the windscreen. By pulling a lever on the mirror the driver can cut out dazzle from the headlamps of following cars.

DRAWING BOARD TO SHOWROOM

Before a car can even begin to take shape on the designer's drawing board the company has to decide exactly what type of car to make. Should it be simple, to sell a large number cheaply? Or luxurious, to sell a few at a higher price? Should it be a hatchback, a sports car or a saloon? Once they have decided they give a "brief", or outline of their ideas, to the design studio. It may be many years before the car goes on sale, so the stylists must think ahead to keep the car up-to-date. Every piece of the new car is tested on computer, in laboratories, in wind-tunnels (page 33) and on the road. The first cars, known as the "prototypes", are built by hand. Later, the production line starts up for a trial run of 50 or 100. Once these are checked and approved, real production begins, and the showrooms prepare to receive the new car.

A car is born
A new car takes shape amongst felt pens, sticky tape, clay and computers. Apart from the new car, people are working on many different projects. These include "face-lifts" and improvements - such as easier-to-read instruments - for current models, and ideas for show cars or concept cars (pages 62-63).

2 Miniature magic
The chosen design goes next to the modellers. They use fine clay smoothed over a foam block to make a quarter-scale model, which is then spray-painted. Sometimes, to save time and money, just half a model is built. Placed against a mirror, it looks like a complete car.

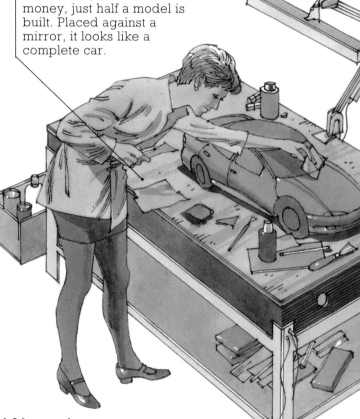

1 Ideas galore
Designers have to create an attractive, streamlined shape which will hold all the working parts of the car and carry the occupants in comfort. Finally, they do a full-size "tape drawing", using black tape on a white wall, to check the dimensions.

Narrowing it down
In a large company, design teams work on several different ideas for the new car at the same time, and may do hundreds of sketches. These are reviewed, discussed and gradually narrowed down until one is selected as the final design.

Designers use felt pens and airbrushes

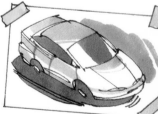

The car must look good from every angle

3 Table-top testing

Computers play an important role in car design. Once the shape is fixed roughly, engineers make a computer image of the new car and all its parts. They use this to check such things as the strength and weight of the car, the size of the interior, and the suspension (pages 34-35). Using the computer, the designers test and change the car even before it is built.

On test

Test drivers spend a year or more in scorching deserts and Arctic snow-fields to check for weak points. They test hand-built prototypes, or "pre-production" vehicles, built on the production line. These are all scrapped after testing, or smashed in safety trials (pages 28-29). Manufacturers try hard to keep the new model a secret until it is launched to the public. During testing, they disguise the shape with paint, cardboard and fibreglass panels. They even glue false badges on to confuse "spies" sent from car newspapers and magazines.

A fibreglass panel turns this saloon into an estate car

4 Paint and clay

The technicians build a full-size clay model, or "buck". It is then painted - including the "windows", which are painted black. A computer records its exact measurements. The finished car will be based on these - so the buck must be accurate.

Once painted, the clay model looks very realistic

Clay is spread over a wood and foam frame

Streamlining is always important (pages 32-33)

The same, but different

Compare this scene with the factory building Model T Fords on page 14. Eighty years after the Model T was first made, car factories still use the same assembly-line idea. But things have changed, and there are no longer separate lines to assemble the body and the chassis, or car frame (page 34). Car factories today are very clean. They have more machines, including robots, and fewer people. Parts arrive at the assembly line on driverless trolleys.

6 Paintbox

The car is spray-painted by robots. They are ideal for this job, because the paints can damage people's lungs. The opening panels - doors, bonnet and boot-lid - are propped open so that the paint spray can get into every corner. This area of the factory must be extra-clean to prevent dust spoiling the finish. Afterwards the car rolls through a heated tunnel, or "oven", to dry the paint.

5 Kit of parts

A car's basic bodyshell is made of many panels. Huge machines stamp the panels out of flat sheets of steel. After trimming, robot trolleys carry these to the assembly line. The inner sides and roof are welded on to the floorpan (page 34). Then the outer panels are added, to make a rigid shell.

The clay model is an exact replica of the car that is to be made on the production line

The assembly line takes the cars through the various stages of production

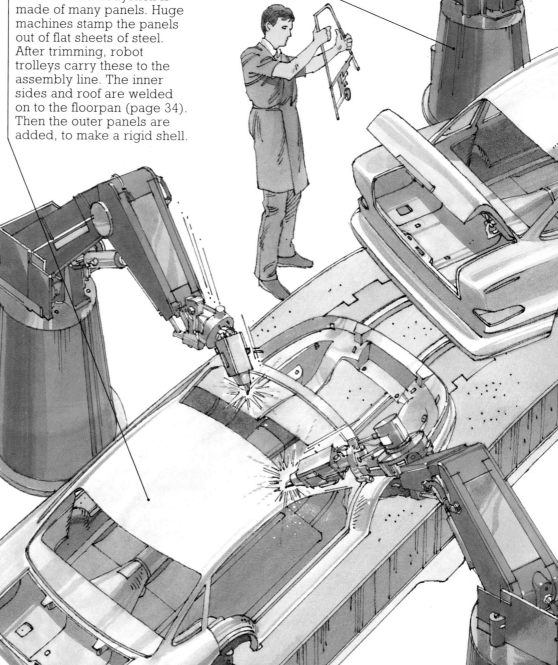

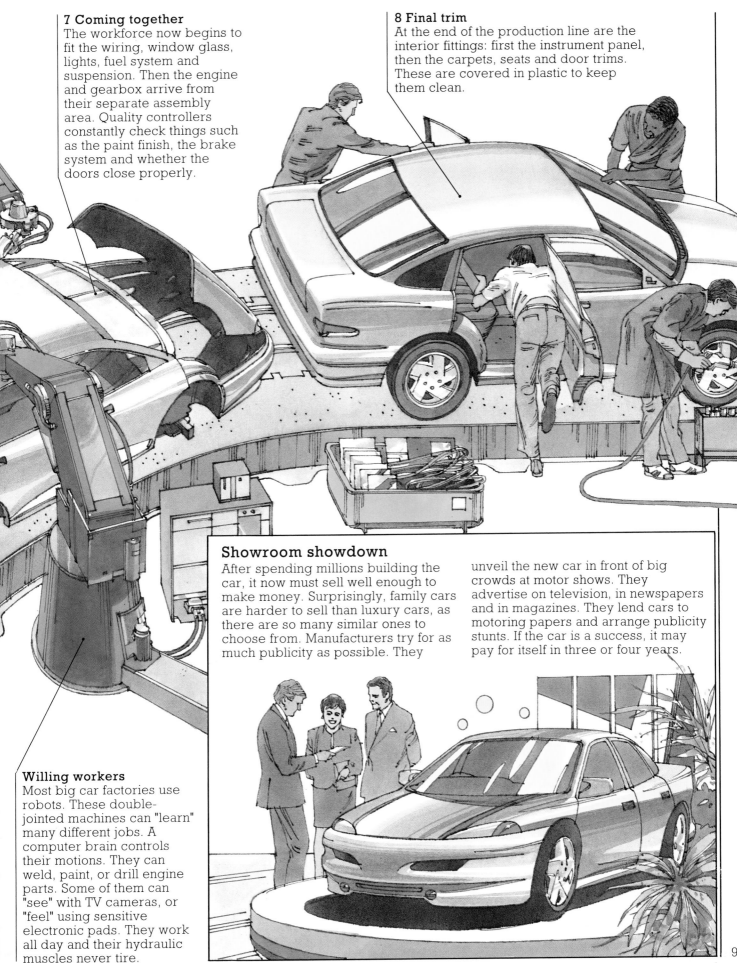

7 Coming together

The workforce now begins to fit the wiring, window glass, lights, fuel system and suspension. Then the engine and gearbox arrive from their separate assembly area. Quality controllers constantly check things such as the paint finish, the brake system and whether the doors close properly.

8 Final trim

At the end of the production line are the interior fittings: first the instrument panel, then the carpets, seats and door trims. These are covered in plastic to keep them clean.

Showroom showdown

After spending millions building the car, it now must sell well enough to make money. Surprisingly, family cars are harder to sell than luxury cars, as there are so many similar ones to choose from. Manufacturers try for as much publicity as possible. They unveil the new car in front of big crowds at motor shows. They advertise on television, in newspapers and in magazines. They lend cars to motoring papers and arrange publicity stunts. If the car is a success, it may pay for itself in three or four years.

Willing workers

Most big car factories use robots. These double-jointed machines can "learn" many different jobs. A computer brain controls their motions. They can weld, paint, or drill engine parts. Some of them can "see" with TV cameras, or "feel" using sensitive electronic pads. They work all day and their hydraulic muscles never tire.

THE ENGINE

At the heart of the motor car lies the engine, which produces the power that moves the car. The principles of the modern petrol engine remain the same as they were over a century ago. It is still driven by internal combustion (page 12) and burns fuel, usually a mixture of petrol and air. Each cylinder goes through the four-stroke cycle - a sequence of actions that occurs over and over again to create power. The difference is that today's engine is far more reliable, uses far less fuel, and is quieter and smoother. However, problems with pollution and dwindling petrol supplies have led to experiments with alternatives to the petrol engine. But almost everyone driving a car at this moment is sitting behind a four-stroke piston engine.

Hidden power

Inside the engine hundreds of parts are busy turning petrol into movement. At the engine's centre, fierce explosions of fuel drive the pistons up and down. These drive the crankshaft which turns the clutch, gearbox and wheels. At the top, the valves snap open and shut, providing fuel to the pistons. All these parts fit into the "block", or engine casing, which is honeycombed with water- and oil-ways.

Distributor

Each cylinder must fire in turn. All four spark plugs are connected to a rotating switch called the distributor. This connects them, one after another, to the coil. The coil turns the low voltage of the battery into very high voltage. The wire coil creates a spark in the plug which explodes the fuel in the cylinder.

Spark-plug leads

Cylinder

Piston

A filter keeps the oil clean as it flows around the engine

Carburetter

The carburetter controls the mixture of petrol and air that feeds the engine. It relies on the suction of the pistons to pull fuel in with the air. The inlet has a very narrow part, the "venturi", where the suction is strongest. Air rushing past sucks the fuel through a tiny hole from a fuel bowl. The faster the air, the more fuel goes in. The mixture forms a burnable vapour.

Air inlet

Fuel bowl

Venturi

Fuel inlet pipe

Spark plug

Float and valve control fuel level

Throttle valve

Fuel injection

An alternative, more efficient, system is fuel injection. A small pump squirts petrol directly into the air inlet through an injector nozzle. A computer chip measures how hard the engine is working and adjusts the fuel flow to match.

Spark plug

Inlet valve

Air inlet

Injector nozzle

Piston

The oil pump is fixed to the distributor shaft

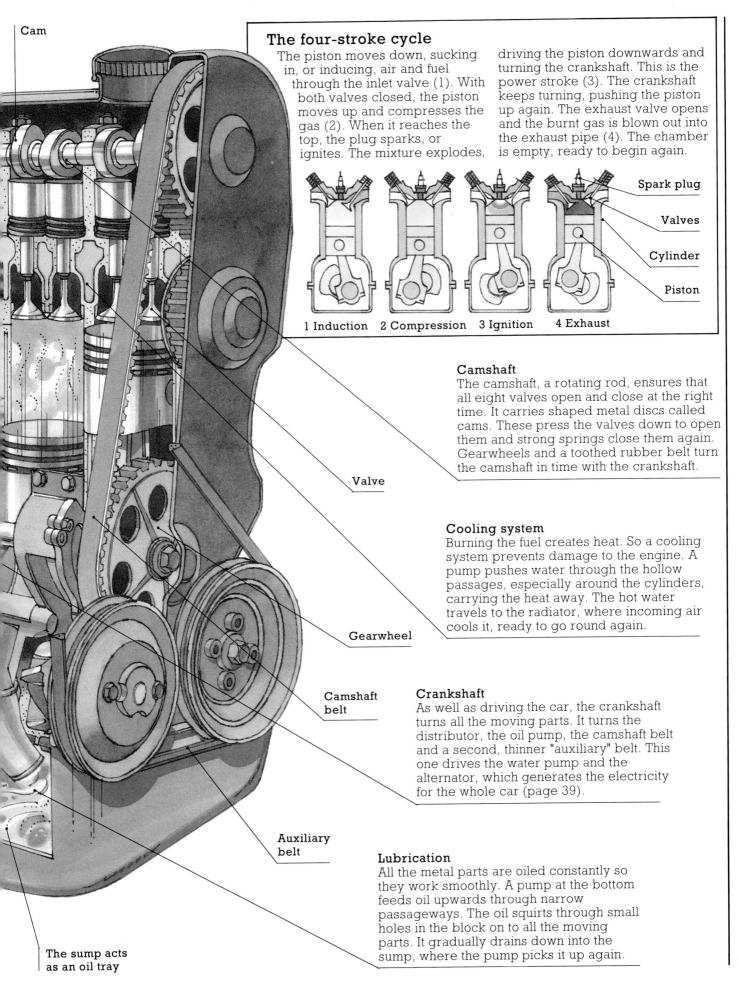

Cam

The four-stroke cycle

The piston moves down, sucking in, or inducing, air and fuel through the inlet valve (1). With both valves closed, the piston moves up and compresses the gas (2). When it reaches the top, the plug sparks, or ignites. The mixture explodes, driving the piston downwards and turning the crankshaft. This is the power stroke (3). The crankshaft keeps turning, pushing the piston up again. The exhaust valve opens and the burnt gas is blown out into the exhaust pipe (4). The chamber is empty, ready to begin again.

Spark plug

Valves

Cylinder

Piston

1 Induction   2 Compression   3 Ignition   4 Exhaust

Camshaft

The camshaft, a rotating rod, ensures that all eight valves open and close at the right time. It carries shaped metal discs called cams. These press the valves down to open them and strong springs close them again. Gearwheels and a toothed rubber belt turn the camshaft in time with the crankshaft.

Valve

Cooling system

Burning the fuel creates heat. So a cooling system prevents damage to the engine. A pump pushes water through the hollow passages, especially around the cylinders, carrying the heat away. The hot water travels to the radiator, where incoming air cools it, ready to go round again.

Gearwheel

Camshaft belt

Crankshaft

As well as driving the car, the crankshaft turns all the moving parts. It turns the distributor, the oil pump, the camshaft belt and a second, thinner "auxiliary" belt. This one drives the water pump and the alternator, which generates the electricity for the whole car (page 39).

Auxiliary belt

Lubrication

All the metal parts are oiled constantly so they work smoothly. A pump at the bottom feeds oil upwards through narrow passageways. The oil squirts through small holes in the block on to all the moving parts. It gradually drains down into the sump, where the pump picks it up again.

The sump acts as an oil tray

THE FIRST CAR

The first carriages to run without horses were powered by steam. Nicholas Cugnot in France and Richard Trevithick in England built experimental road vehicles, and by the 1840s there were regular steam coaches running to and from London. But they were bulky and complicated, and damaged the roads. In 1859 a Belgian called Etienne Lenoir perfected a new, lighter type of engine. It burned its fuel, coal-gas, inside the cylinder - a process called internal combustion - instead of burning coal outside a steam boiler. Later, Nicholas Otto devised the four-stroke cycle (page 11), making more powerful engines possible. By this time petrol, a much easier fuel to use than coal-gas, had been produced in the United States. When vehicles were built that combined this new technology with the right fuel - petrol - the motor car was off to a racing start.

Race to succeed

Cugnot's gun carriage of 1769 was the first self-powered vehicle, and later steam carriages became very popular. Marcus' machine of 1874 proved a non-starter, but when Daimler and Benz climbed on to their inventions of 1885-86, the motor age had dawned.

Gun carriage
Cugnot's *Cabriot* was built to pull heavy guns. The big copper boiler sent steam to two pistons on the front wheel. However, it crashed into a wall on its first run.

Marcus' upright steering wheel was one of the first of its kind

Steam for two
Britain's Thomas Ricketts had the bright idea of building a small steam vehicle in 1858. There was room for two people in the front, and a stoker crouched at the back. Before that, steam buses and trains were common, but only carriages pulled by horses were used for private transport.

Almost there
This car was running in 1874 in Vienna, Austria. Because it had a four-stroke engine and four wheels, some people call it the first car. But it ran on coal-gas, not petrol, so it could never have become an efficient vehicle. Local people complained about the noise of its crude engine and iron tyres, and its builder, Siegfried Marcus, gave up the project.

Rolling ahead

While Daimler used heavy carriage wheels, Benz chose lightweight, spoked wheels. At first, all wheels had solid tyres of metal or rubber, until John Dunlop patented the pneumatic or air-filled tyre in 1888. Strong wire-spoked wheels became standard in the 1930s, but were expensive. Steel disc wheels, which were cheap and light, were introduced in the 1940s. Today's sports cars and luxury saloons have light, strong, cast-alloy wheels.

Spoked wheel, 1900

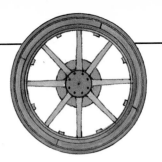

Wooden wheel, 1905

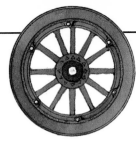

Steel-spoked, 1925

Wire-spoked, 1935

Pressed steel, 1945

Cast alloy, 1990

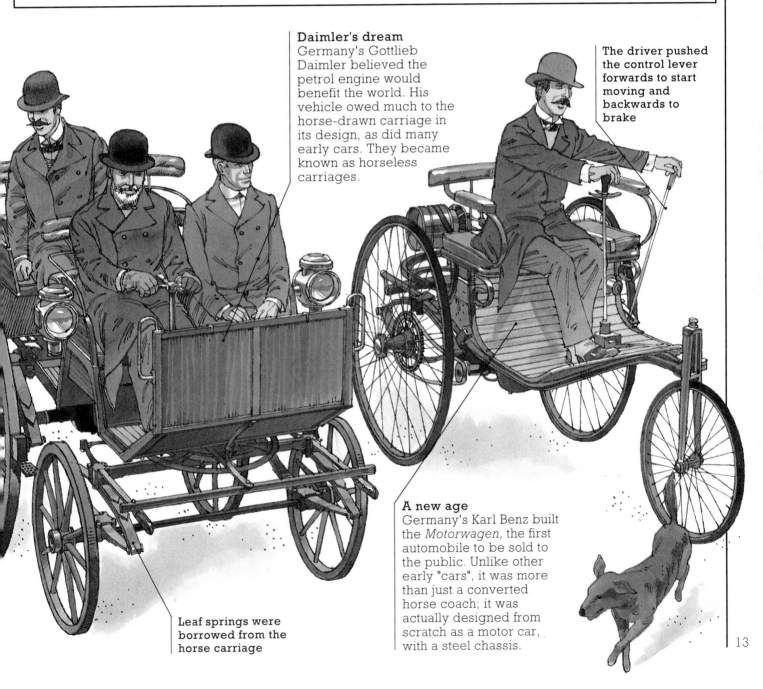

Daimler's dream
Germany's Gottlieb Daimler believed the petrol engine would benefit the world. His vehicle owed much to the horse-drawn carriage in its design, as did many early cars. They became known as horseless carriages.

The driver pushed the control lever forwards to start moving and backwards to brake

A new age
Germany's Karl Benz built the *Motorwagen*, the first automobile to be sold to the public. Unlike other early "cars", it was more than just a converted horse coach; it was actually designed from scratch as a motor car, with a steel chassis.

Leaf springs were borrowed from the horse carriage

CARS FOR EVERYONE

In 1902 a young mechanic in the United States founded a motor company bearing his own name. It became one of the most famous names in the world - Ford. And the Model T became the most famous Ford car. Henry Ford wanted to build affordable cars so that every family could have one. In 1908 he invented the "assembly line" system, which meant that many cars were put together at the same time. This way he could build cars more cheaply than anyone else. Unlike his rivals he offered only one model, which kept prices down. The Model T started at $850 in 1909, but seven years later it was down to just $260! Within a few years Ford doubled the number of cars in the United States. Factories in Britain, Germany and Australia also built the Model T, or "Tin Lizzie" as people called it. Ford had built 15 million by the time he stopped making it in 1927.

Down the line
In Ford's Highland Park factory in Detroit the assembly line never stopped. Workers added parts to the car body which was then dropped on to the chassis below. Each car took 1¹/₂ hours to assemble, and a new Model T rolled out of the factory every 40 seconds.

Easy changes
The Model T's four-cylinder engine was simple but not powerful. It could reach speeds of 64kph (40mph). The car had an unusual gearbox, with only two gears. The driver changed from low to high gear by pushing a pedal. This was easier than changing gear by hand. The driver controlled the speed with a lever on the steering wheel.

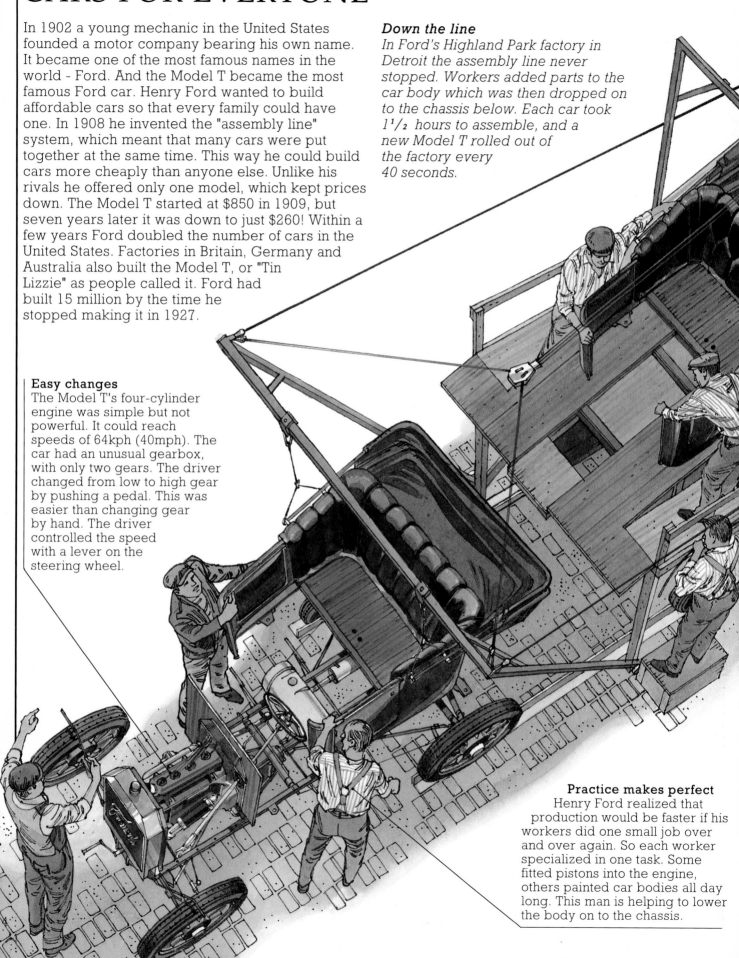

Practice makes perfect
Henry Ford realized that production would be faster if his workers did one small job over and over again. So each worker specialized in one task. Some fitted pistons into the engine, others painted car bodies all day long. This man is helping to lower the body on to the chassis.

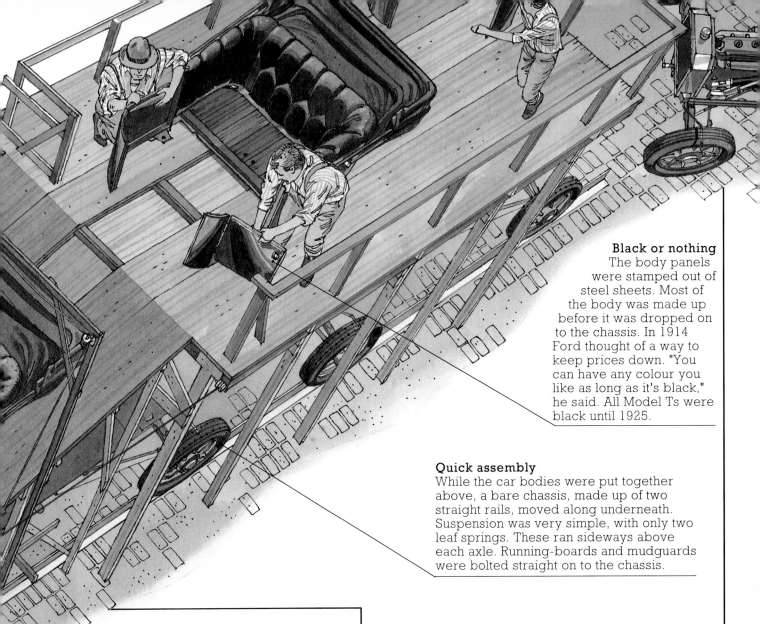

Black or nothing
The body panels were stamped out of steel sheets. Most of the body was made up before it was dropped on to the chassis. In 1914 Ford thought of a way to keep prices down. "You can have any colour you like as long as it's black," he said. All Model Ts were black until 1925.

Quick assembly
While the car bodies were put together above, a bare chassis, made up of two straight rails, moved along underneath. Suspension was very simple, with only two leaf springs. These ran sideways above each axle. Running-boards and mudguards were bolted straight on to the chassis.

"My Merry Oldsmobile"
Ford pioneered the moving assembly line, but he was not the first to mass-produce a car. In 1902, Ransom Olds introduced his two-seat buggy in the United States, and made many thousands of them. Called the Curved-dash Oldsmobile, it had a tiny engine under its simple but stylish body with its curved dashboard. There were two gears, and a lever to steer with.

Oldsmobile - 1903

Familiar face
The Model T was easily recognizable throughout the United States. There were only a few body styles, and the basic design changed little from 1908 to 1927. This had both good and bad results for the Ford company. Though the Model T grew cheaper and so remained popular, its slow engine and open body allowed rival makes to overtake it in terms of comfort and speed.

The Doctor's Coupé of 1917 was one of the few closed-in cars Ford offered

The four-seat tourer of 1927 was one of the last of the Model Ts

15

CLASSIC CARS

What do we mean when we call a car a "classic"? To some people, only valuable cars deserve the name. Others feel that all cars of a certain age are classics. Twenty years ago a car might have been scrapped because it was out of date, but not today, as old cars are back in fashion. People can still buy new parts for cars which are over 60 years old and even a wreck can be turned into a gleaming show-piece. Many old cars now run faster and better than they did in their youth. There are races, rallies and tours for all ages of cars. The oldest and best-known is the London to Brighton Run, introduced in 1896 to celebrate the date when anti-motoring laws were dropped in Britain.

Old but modern
France quickly took over from Germany as the centre of automobile design in the early 1900s. De Dion's 1903 Model Q was one of the first vehicles built that we would recognize as a car today. It had a steering wheel, a front bonnet covering the simple engine, and rear-wheel drive. It was cheap, reliable and very popular.

Classic collection
Some museums collect cars of one make, such as the Duesenberg Museum, Indiana, USA. Others try to show a little of everything, such as the National Motor Museum at Beaulieu, England. The cars shown here are not the fastest, or the most expensive. But they do show how cars developed through the years. Even ordinary cars can change history.

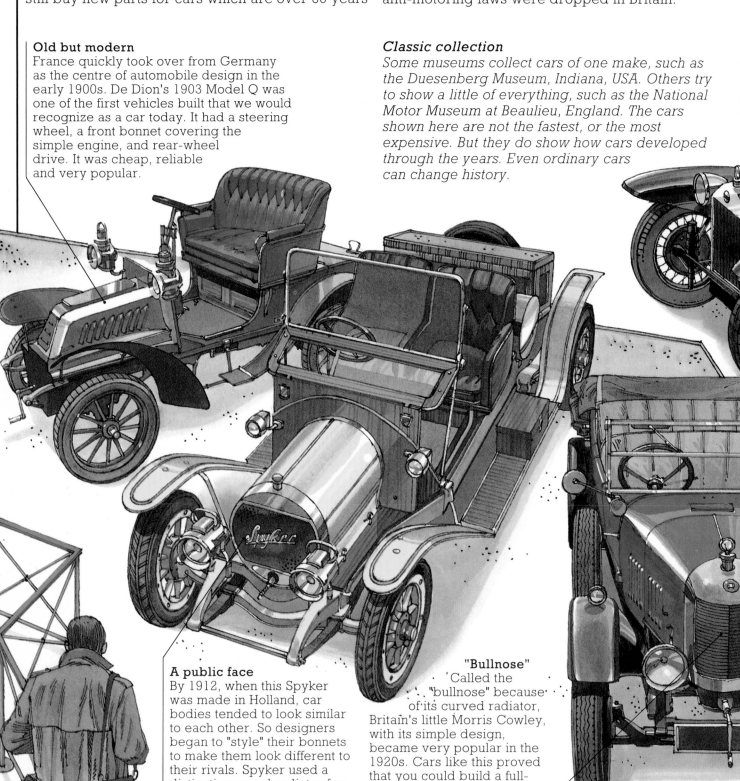

A public face
By 1912, when this Spyker was made in Holland, car bodies tended to look similar to each other. So designers began to "style" their bonnets to make them look different to their rivals. Spyker used a distinctive round radiator for its high quality cars.

"Bullnose"
Called the "bullnose" because of its curved radiator, Britain's little Morris Cowley, with its simple design, became very popular in the 1920s. Cars like this proved that you could build a full-size family car at a low price.

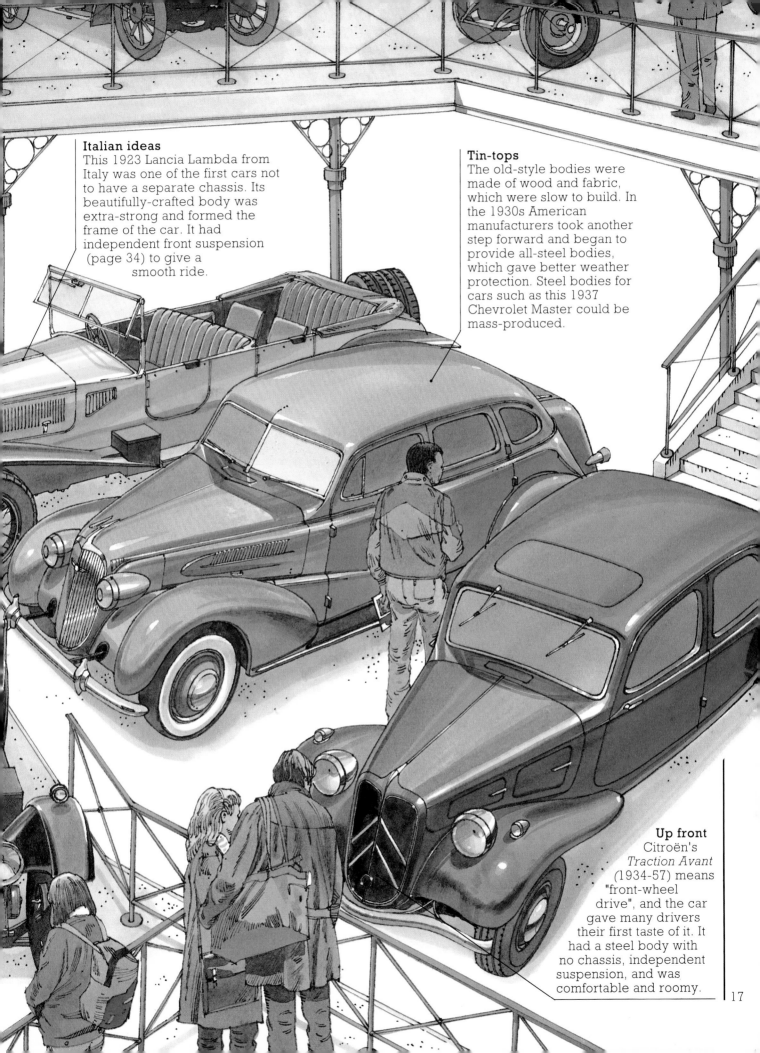

Italian ideas
This 1923 Lancia Lambda from Italy was one of the first cars not to have a separate chassis. Its beautifully-crafted body was extra-strong and formed the frame of the car. It had independent front suspension (page 34) to give a smooth ride.

Tin-tops
The old-style bodies were made of wood and fabric, which were slow to build. In the 1930s American manufacturers took another step forward and began to provide all-steel bodies, which gave better weather protection. Steel bodies for cars such as this 1937 Chevrolet Master could be mass-produced.

Up front
Citroën's *Traction Avant* (1934-57) means "front-wheel drive", and the car gave many drivers their first taste of it. It had a steel body with no chassis, independent suspension, and was comfortable and roomy.

17

TRAVELLING IN STYLE

In the early 1900s motorists suffered many hazards we do not have to face today. Roads were not tarmacked, but were rough and unmade. Stones and pot-holes made driving uncomfortable and caused endless punctures. When it rained, the roads turned to mud, and cars skidded or became stuck. Breakdowns were frequent, and drivers had to know how to repair their cars. Even petrol was hard to find. At first it had to be bought in tins from chemists' shops. There was also the problem of other road-users: not cars - it was rare to meet another one - but pedestrians, cyclists, dogs and cattle. They were not used to cars and did not realize how fast they could travel, so accidents were frequent. Many people disliked cars because of the noise, the smell, and the dangers they brought.

Tough travellers
Pioneer motorists had to be hardy and enthusiastic. The simple, open bodywork of most cars gave little protection from the wind, rain and dust, so clothing had to be warm and rainproof. This led to some weird and wonderful creations.

Horses were much more common than breakdown trucks - here a horse comes to the rescue of a car that has stalled in a ford

Riding hood
Women wore silk veils or hoods over their hats to protect them from the dust and wind. This pink hood has a clear window to peer through. The elderly woman's fur coat has a thick collar to protect her neck.

Roadside repairs
This Lorraine-De Dietrich has detachable wheels. The fresh tyre is fitted to a spare wheel, making it easy to swap the wheels over. This is much quicker than trying to repair a puncture. The driver is wearing goggles and a cap with ear-flaps. His "umbrella coat" has a tight rubber neck to stop water getting in.

Smart and simple
The couple stuck in the water are wearing the simplest motoring outfits. A heavy coat and cap keep the man warm. The woman wears a veil to keep her bonnet on her head, and a thick rug tucked around her legs.

Sprag snag
Early brakes were not reliable. To stop the car rolling back on a hill, the driver released a "sprag" - a rod which hung below the car and stuck into the road. If released when the car was moving, it could flip the vehicle over!

A "snuggery" completely enclosed the passenger's legs and feet

Leather gauntlets

Back-to-front
This man wears his reversible cap with the goggles at the back. He can turn it around and flip down the goggles when they set off. The driver's hood has ear-flaps, hooded eye-pieces and a "beak" to avoid breathing in dust.

The coat has a tight-fitting collar to keep out the rain

Canine costume
It was not only humans who wore bizarre costumes to protect them from the hazards of early motoring. In Paris, in 1903, motorists could buy a leather coat, hood and goggles for their pet dog.

LUXURY CARS

Luxury means more than having a television in your car. True luxury cars are made from the highest quality materials and put together with great care - not just the lavish fittings on the outside, but also the engine and mechanical systems inside the car. In the early years cars were a time-consuming pastime, not a reliable means of transport. Motoring was a rich person's hobby. Car manufacturers constantly tried to improve the quality and reliability of their cars. This quality reached its peak in the 1930s with makes such as Bugatti, Duesenberg and Hispano-Suiza. Craftsmen hand-built these vehicles, often to an owner's special requirements. Today's luxury cars are machine-built, though they may be finished by hand.

Riding in luxury
Although very different in looks and period, both the British Rolls-Royce Silver Ghost (early 1900s), with its hand-crafted coach work, and the American Cadillac (1990s), with its expensive fittings, offer comfort with style.

Home, James!
When having servants was common, wealthy motorists would employ a chauffeur to maintain, repair and drive their car. He often had to wait for hours outside the theatre or the station until his master or mistress was ready to go home, and he was expected to clean the car every night before he went to bed.

Flying power
Many car manufacturers have also built aero-engines. Rolls-Royce built a high-powered engine for the Supermarine S6B sea-plane. This led to the famous Merlin engine which powered the Spitfire and the Hurricane fighters in the Second World War (1939-45). Today, Rolls-Royce jets power many airliners, including Boeing 747s and Concorde.

The supermarine S6B won the Schneider Trophy in 1929

Folding "Cape-cart" hood

The high-quality six-cylinder engine was smooth and reliable

Simply the best
Rolls-Royce caused a sensation when they launched their new model in 1906. It was fast and beautifully made, and was the smoothest car yet built. Within a few years it earned the reputation of being "the best car in the world". It earned the name "Silver Ghost" because of its quiet engine and aluminium body.

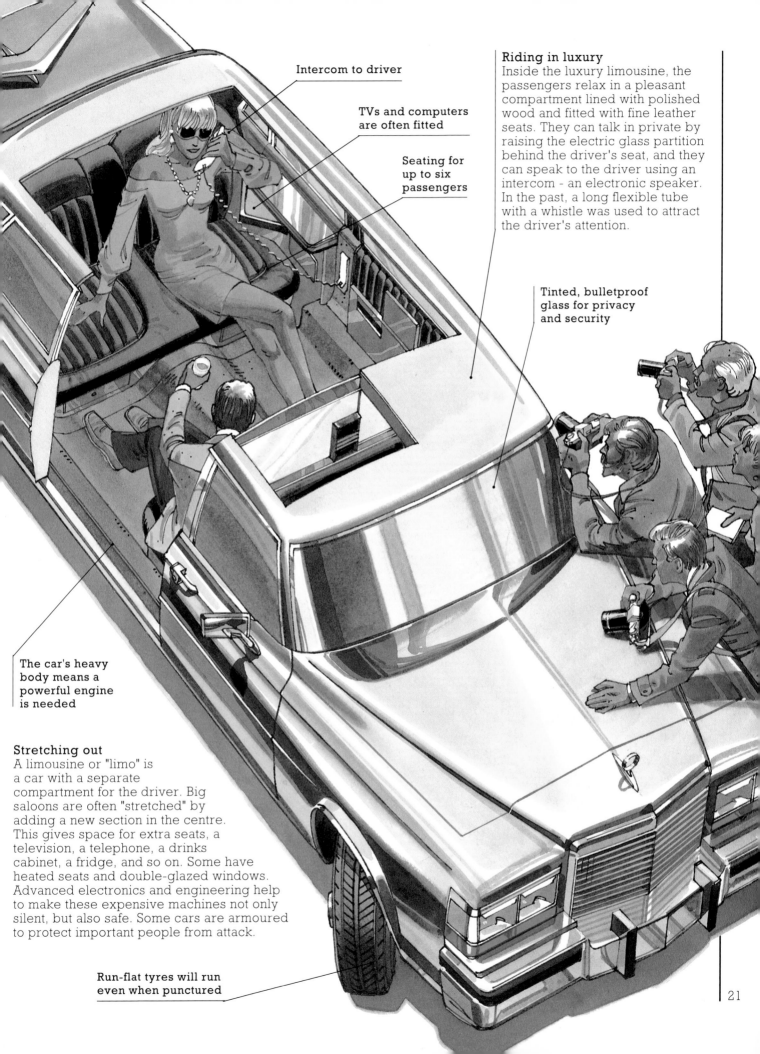

Intercom to driver

TVs and computers
are often fitted

Seating for
up to six
passengers

Riding in luxury
Inside the luxury limousine, the
passengers relax in a pleasant
compartment lined with polished
wood and fitted with fine leather
seats. They can talk in private by
raising the electric glass partition
behind the driver's seat, and they
can speak to the driver using an
intercom - an electronic speaker.
In the past, a long flexible tube
with a whistle was used to attract
the driver's attention.

Tinted, bulletproof
glass for privacy
and security

The car's heavy
body means a
powerful engine
is needed

Stretching out
A limousine or "limo" is
a car with a separate
compartment for the driver. Big
saloons are often "stretched" by
adding a new section in the centre.
This gives space for extra seats, a
television, a telephone, a drinks
cabinet, a fridge, and so on. Some have
heated seats and double-glazed windows.
Advanced electronics and engineering help
to make these expensive machines not only
silent, but also safe. Some cars are armoured
to protect important people from attack.

Run-flat tyres will run
even when punctured

THE AMERICAN WAY

During the 1950s and 1960s cars dominated American life and culture. Quick to recover after the Second World War (1939-45), companies soon switched from building tanks to making cars. The early 1950s were exciting, prosperous years of new discoveries and inventions. People wanted to show that they were well-off, so they preferred large, impressive cars to smaller models. Car sales increased rapidly, reaching a peak in 1955. Car manufacturers brought out new, showier models each year, with more chrome-plated fittings, electric gadgets and decorative fins. Once a car was two years old, it looked completely out of date! These cars were perfect for life in the United States, but only a few were sold abroad.

The car is king
This is a scene from a small, thriving American town in 1957. Cars had so captured the public's imagination that people could shop, dine and watch films from the comfort of their own cars. Cars were no longer simply a means of getting from place to place. Owning a big, flashy car was also a way of saying that you were successful.

Burgers on wheels
Fast food was an American speciality, and hamburgers were everyone's favourite. Drive-in burger bars could be found across the whole country. You drove up to a window, gave your order through a microphone, and then drove on to another window. Almost as soon as you got there, the food was ready to be collected and eaten.

Service on skates
In some burger bars and drive-in cinemas the food was brought to the car. A waitress on roller-skates has brought trays of food to hang on the doors of this 1953 Buick Skylark convertible, which had smooth lines, a distinctive radiator grille, and could carry six people.

The 1957 Cadillac Coupé de Ville was almost 5.5m (18ft) long, with a smooth, eight-cylinder engine

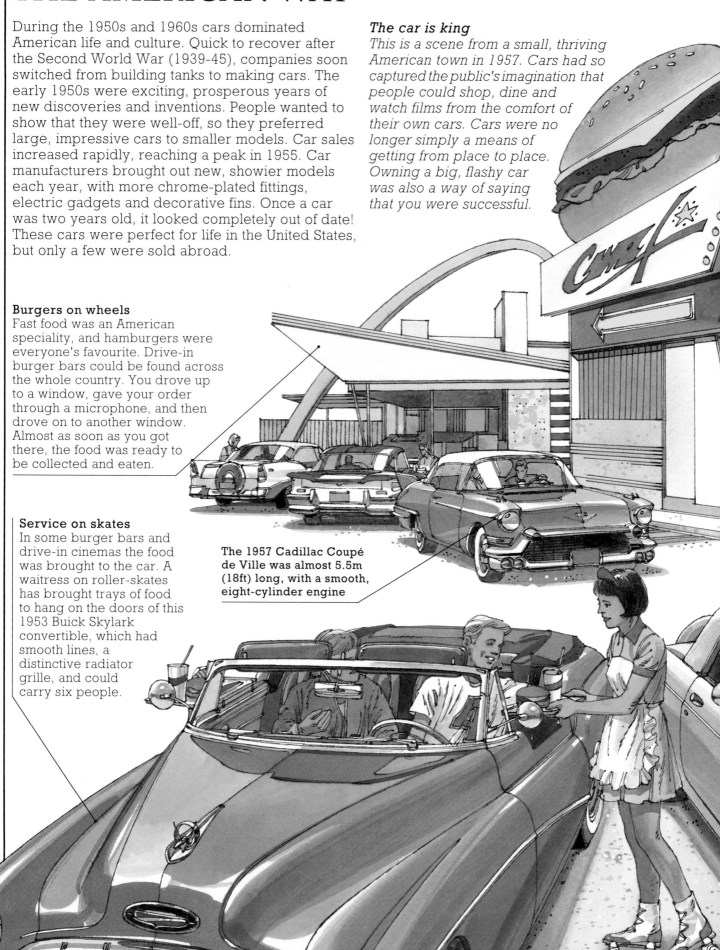

Grocery garage
It was not just fast food that was delivered straight to the car - it was even possible to buy groceries at drive-in supermarkets without having to open the car door. Shoppers placed their orders through the car window. Attendants brought the groceries to the counter, where the customers paid for them before leaving.

Supersigns
Restaurants, motels and shops realized that there was a lot of money to be made from passing motorists. As cars sped by on the main street, huge advertisements competed to catch the drivers' eyes. The cut-out cars, giant hot-dogs, larger-than-life cows and flashing neon signs all competed to make the biggest impact.

Car hotels
The motel was, and is, another well-known feature of American life. It offered travellers cheap and plain lodgings after a long day's driving. Guests could drive their car right to the door of their own cabin. The motel had no dining room, but there were usually fast food places nearby to satisfy hungry appetites.

Injected style
This 1957 Chevrolet Bel Air Hardtop came with a fuel-injected engine (page 10). It was fast, stylish and cheap. In the mid-1950s, Chevrolet produced many famous models, such as the Corvette (page 24).

The Thunderbird - Ford's two-seater rival to the Corvette - had a simple, attractive shape and a lift-off hardtop

23

Living in America

For American teenagers living in a small town in the 1950s, cars were important fashion items. If they could not afford the latest Chevrolet, they altered - or "customized" - an old Ford, adding chrome fittings, larger wheels or even a new engine. Young people fine-tuned their cars and raced them, usually two at a time, on the outskirts of town. This "drag racing" became very popular - but it was also illegal. Today's drag racers (page 43) are specially-built cars that look very different from the family saloons used for drag racing in the 1950s.

Spoilt for choice
American cars of the 1950s were not built to last, and manufacturers changed their models each year. When the new designs appeared, owners traded their old cars in for new ones. This meant that every town had huge "car lots" that sold large numbers of cheap, second-hand cars.

Highway cruiser
The drag-racers had to keep an eye out for police patrol cars. They were usually big, powerful saloons like this 1956 Ford, with loud chrome sirens on the roof. Patrol cars often cruised the streets, watching for trouble.

All-American sportster
Chevrolet's Corvette was the first mass-produced American sports car. It had a fibreglass body and a powerful engine, and was small and simple inside - more like a European sports car than an American one.

Hot rod
Plain family cars were often customized into "hot rod" racers, such as this Model A Ford. Hot rods had skinny tyres at the front, fat ones at the back and large engines. Some had their bonnet and wings removed to make them light and fast.

24

Bonnet sculpture

The 1950s produced many stylish bonnet mascots. Some were based on the badge of the car, such as the Pontiac "Tin Indian"; others were copied from aircraft designs and looked like missiles or propellers.

1949 Buick   Pontiac "Tin Indian"   Pontiac Silver Streak

At the drive-in cinema, every car was given a plug-in loudspeaker so people could listen to the widescreen movie

Elegant Eldorado

In the early 1950s Cadillac stopped producing its cheaper models and launched its luxurious Eldorado range. Long, low and wide, this 1956 Cadillac Eldorado was one of the most expensive cars on the market, combining comfort with power.

Fast fins

The clean-cut lines of this 1957 Chrysler New Yorker convertible made it stand out from the crowd. It had a curved windscreen, and huge, pointed tail-fins which were a fashion craze at this time. Car manufacturers competed to add the tallest and longest fins to their cars.

Flip-top lid

Drivers liked convertibles, but they did not like having to fold back the flimsy canvas roof by hand. In 1957 Ford produced the Fairlane Skyliner. It had a steel roof which automatically folded away into the boot at the press of a button. Although this four-seater car looked huge from the outside, there was very little room in the back or in the boot, because the space was required for the roof mechanism's motors and wiring.

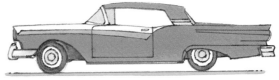

With the roof in place, the Skyliner looked like an ordinary saloon

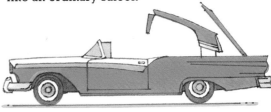

It took about a minute for the roof to fold back into the boot

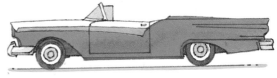

The result - an open-topped cruiser

25

SPORTS CARS

Sports cars are built for speed. They are fun to drive and stylish in design. To most people a sports car means an open-topped two-seater. Yet there are closed sports cars. That they look good and can be driven fast is more important than the number of passengers they carry. As early as 1910 car manufacturers realized that while some people just wanted a reliable car, others wanted speed. By the 1920s sports cars began to look quite different to touring cars. They had big, powerful engines which hid under long bonnets and the driver sat near the rear wheels. This meant the car could turn corners more easily. In the 1960s the Italian firm Lamborghini followed the "mid-engined" racing car idea (page 5). Modern sports cars may have their engines in the front, middle or rear, but they all have one important ingredient - fun for two.

Years apart
Tyres spinning, engines revving, a parade of sports cars of different ages streaks along winding mountain roads. Sleek modern coupés mix with upright old two-seaters on roads that are hard work for the older cars with their thin tyres and weak brakes.

Setting a trend
The Prince Henry Vauxhall was one of the first sports cars. It was named after the Prince Henry Trials of 1910. This British car achieved 121kph (75mph) before the First World War (1914-18). It was easily recognized by its pointed nose, and by the bonnet flutes, which Vauxhall used on all its cars until the 1960s.

Split wind-screen

Speed with style
Alfa Romeo confirmed the Italian flair for speed with the 1750 Gran Sport. It won the famous Mille Miglia road race twice, in 1929 and 1930. It had a powerful engine, and could reach 153kph (95mph). Most models had beautiful two-seater bodywork. It was the most successful racing name before the Second World War (1939-45).

Cheap and cheerful
Made in 1928, the first British MG Midget was a small car with a small engine, borrowed from a Morris saloon. It had a light two-seater body. The Midget proved that sports cars could offer style and fun without being expensive.

Behind the wheel

This is a driver's view of an Austin-Healey, a typical British sports car of the 1960s. It has a polished wooden dashboard, a stubby gearlever, and a wooden steering wheel. The controls and the heating are simple. For years enthusiasts wanted cockpits to look like this. Today, safety comes first. Designers use plastic instead of wood to reduce injuries in a crash.

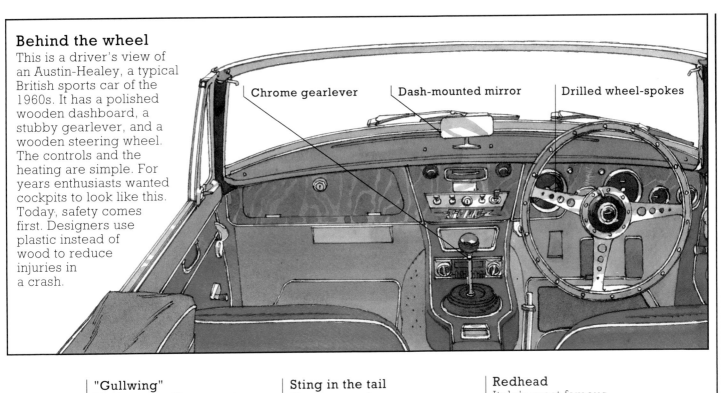

Chrome gearlever

Dash-mounted mirror

Drilled wheel-spokes

"Gullwing"
Designed in Germany in 1952, the Mercedes-Benz 300SL had a light but strong tubular steel frame. Because the sides of the chassis were very high it had "gullwing" doors, hinged in the roof, that swung upwards when opened. It reached speeds of 232kph (144mph).

Sting in the tail
German engineer Ferdinand Porsche designed many vehicles, from tanks to racing cars. The most famous, apart from the Volkswagen, is the rear-engined Porsche. He built the first one in 1948, using a VW engine. The six-cylinder version, the 911, arrived in 1964.

Redhead
Italy's most famous products are red Ferraris. Most have two seats and carry little luggage. But they are beautiful and fast and have a fine racing history. Called *Testarossa* (Redhead) because of its engine's red cylinder heads, this Ferrari can do 290kph (180mph).

Softtop roof for open-air motoring

SAFETY FIRST

Accident rates have gone down steadily during the last 40 years or so, but any car journey presents some risk. Vehicle designers work hard to reduce the dangers. It is possible to help prevent crashes by the fitting of simple, comfortable controls and good brakes. Today, electronics can be used to prevent brakes locking and to stop the car skidding. They also give warning of mechanical problems and even check tyre pressures while the car is moving. If a crash should happen, cars are made as strong and as safe as possible to withstand it. Wearing seat-belts and putting children in safety-seats can save lives and reduce injuries. Road planners also have a part to play. Smooth roads, simple junctions and clear signposting reduce the likelihood of accidents.

Hand-operated bulb horn, 1920s

Audible warning
All vehicles are fitted with a warning device. Today, this is usually an electric horn, but bells, gongs and even exhaust-operated whistles have been used. Some luxury cars used to have two horns - a quiet one for use in town and a loud one for the country.

Foot-operated bell, early 1900s

Two-tone air horns, 1960s onwards

Destruction test
Cars with dummies strapped inside are deliberately crashed into concrete blocks at special testing grounds to see how they will react in a crash. Engineers film this in slow-motion so that they can see where to make improvements.

Rear belts, required by law in many countries

Dummies are fitted with sensors

Safety engineers often crash two cars together to find out what could happen in an accident

Child safety
Young children need special seats with harnesses to hold them firmly in place. These seats often face backwards, to stop them sliding out. Older children can sit on a "booster cushion", which raises them up so that they can wear the normal seat-belt.

Safety cell
Passengers are surrounded by a very strong "cage" which should protect them even if the car overturns. The door hinges and locks are designed so that they do not burst open during a crash, but open normally to allow escape from the damaged car.

Strapped in

Seat-belts reduce injuries by holding passengers firmly in place if there is a crash. They have to fit properly to work well, resting snugly against the shoulder (not the neck) and below the waist, across the bones of the pelvis. If the lap-belt lies over the stomach it can cause internal injuries.

The blue lines show the correct seat-belt positioning; red is incorrect

Keeping a grip

Inside the rubber casing of a modern tyre, steel or synthetic cords give the tyre its shape. The type of rubber used is important: softer rubber gives better grip but wears out faster. Computers help to plan the exact pattern of the tread on a tyre. The blocks and slits that make up the tread bite into the road and push water aside in rainy conditions. Photographs of the tyre print show how well the tread grips the road.

Cameras snap the print of a tyre on a glass panel

Shallow, broad tyres give good grip

Chains can be clipped on for grip in snow

Tyres fitted with studs bite into icy roads

All cars now use safety glass - either toughened, which shatters into small blunt pieces, or laminated, which cracks but does not break apart

Crumple zone

In a completely rigid car, the passengers would take the whole force of any accident. Instead, the car's front and rear are designed to crumple up and absorb some of the impact of a crash, while the engine is arranged to slide under the car rather than into it.

Engineer

Airbags

Some manufacturers use airbags as well as seat-belts in the front of the car. When an electronic sensor feels an impact, it triggers a gas canister which, in a fraction of a second, inflates a tough plastic balloon in front of the driver and passenger.

Bumpers

All modern cars have bumpers which can resist low-speed knocks without damage. They may be made of steel and rubber, or of moulded plastics that squash up but regain their shape after several hours or collapse on high-speed impact.

CAR CHECK-UP

The days are long gone when a motorist's car was tended by a chauffeur and needed lubrication as often as every 300km (188 miles). Today, every new car arrives with a service book. A service is a regular mechanical "check-up" that includes changing the oil in the engine and gearbox, checking spark plugs and filters, and a "tune up" to make sure the engine runs at its best. The details are recorded in the service book. When the car is sold, the new owner can see from the book that the car has been well looked after. Many cars only need a service every 20,000km (12,500 miles). It can be easy to forget to visit the garage, so some cars have service indicator lights. An electronic circuit counts the kilometres the car covers, and flashes a warning when a service is due.

Service session
Perched high in the air, a car reveals its complicated underside as a mechanic adjusts the steering of this German BMW 325i. Regular servicing is vital to keep a car running efficiently. If it develops a fault or has an accident, a specialist dealer has all the equipment to fix it quickly and make it look like new again.

Protective coat
Underneath, the car is usually covered in underseal. This thick black paint acts as rust-proofing, and protects the floorpan (page 34) from flying stone chips. It reduces the vibration of the metal panels, keeping noise down. Some cars have a moulded plastic liner inside the wheelarch to reduce stone damage.

The gearbox
The engine turns much faster than the car's wheels, so they are linked through a gearbox to slow down the drive. The gearbox contains four or five gears, plus reverse. Between the gearbox and the engine is the clutch, which disconnects the drive briefly while changing gear; the driver moves the gear lever to select a gear.

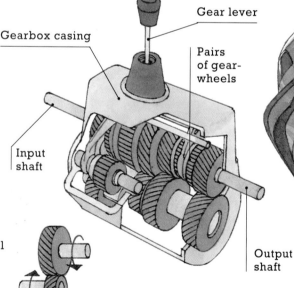

Gear lever

Gearbox casing

Pairs of gear-wheels

Input shaft

Output shaft

Choose your speed
Selecting a gear brings together gearwheels on the input shaft from the engine and the output shaft to the wheels. In low gear (1), the driving gearwheel is smaller than the driven one. This gives more power for starting off and driving up hills, but it uses a lot of fuel. In high gear (2), the gearwheels are closer in size. The car can travel faster but has less power to accelerate.

Breathing out
Escaping exhaust gas is noisy, hot and unhealthy. The exhaust system quietens, cools and cleans it before expelling it through the tail-pipe. The gas is released at tremendous speed and is quietened by a silencer, which either slows the gas down or expands it into a large chamber.

Which way next?

This car uses the "rack and pinion" steering system. A gearwheel at the end of the steering column engages a toothed rack running across the car. Turning the steering wheel slides the rack to left or right. The ends of the rack connect to the steering arms that turn the wheels.

The differential

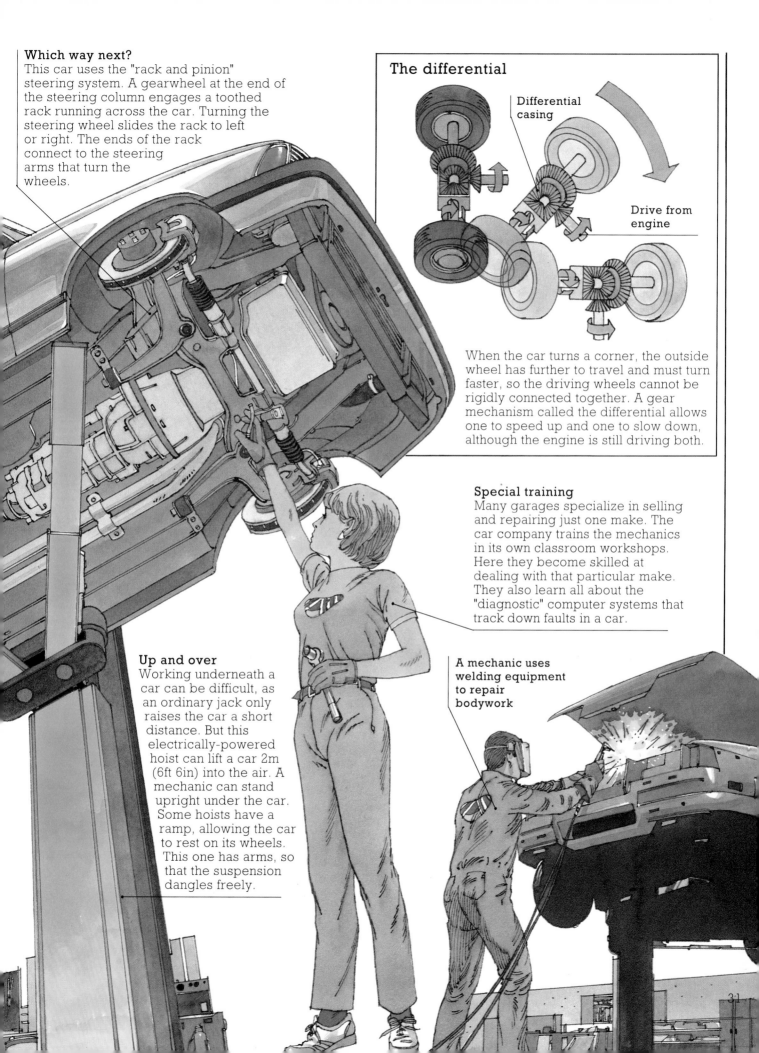

Differential casing

Drive from engine

When the car turns a corner, the outside wheel has further to travel and must turn faster, so the driving wheels cannot be rigidly connected together. A gear mechanism called the differential allows one to speed up and one to slow down, although the engine is still driving both.

Special training

Many garages specialize in selling and repairing just one make. The car company trains the mechanics in its own classroom workshops. Here they become skilled at dealing with that particular make. They also learn all about the "diagnostic" computer systems that track down faults in a car.

Up and over

Working underneath a car can be difficult, as an ordinary jack only raises the car a short distance. But this electrically-powered hoist can lift a car 2m (6ft 6in) into the air. A mechanic can stand upright under the car. Some hoists have a ramp, allowing the car to rest on its wheels. This one has arms, so that the suspension dangles freely.

A mechanic uses welding equipment to repair bodywork

CHANGING SHAPE

Today's cars still run on petrol and have four wheels. Yet they look very different to cars of 80, 50, or even 30 years ago. The biggest change has been in streamlining, or aerodynamics, where a car is designed to move through the air as cleanly as possible. At first, cars were streamlined to make them travel faster on a small engine. Now that we have more powerful engines, cars are streamlined to keep fuel consumption and noise down. Modern cars have steel bodies that no longer need a separate chassis (page 34), so they have become wider and roomier, with simple, flat-sided shapes. But there were advantages to the bulkier shapes of early cars: it was simpler to get in and out of tall cars and the engines were easy to work on. The engines of modern cars are packed under low bonnets, so it is harder to reach all the parts.

Fifty years apart

When Opel built the Kadett in Germany in 1938, speeds were low and petrol was cheap. Streamlining was not so important, so the car was tall. Today's Vauxhall Calibra is built low, wide and smooth to slip through the air at high speeds.

Windscreen fixed by rubber strip

Projecting windscreen wipers

Flip-out indicator

Flush-glazed screen glued into place

Vauxhall Calibra 1990

Breathing in

The Kadett has a tall radiator grille. It needs this to let in a lot of air at lower speeds to cool the engine. Its nose is a complicated shape, with a separate bumper bolted on. The mudguards still look a bit like the old mudguards of the early 1920s, which were fixed on to the car's chassis.

Opel Kadett 1938

Smooth and sleek

Narrow headlamps keep the Calibra's nose low so that air rushes over the top of it. A small radiator opening is enough, because a fan keeps the engine cool even when the car is not moving. Deep plastic bumpers allow only a little air to flow underneath.

Wind tunnels

Cars are tested for "air-drag" in a wind tunnel, where thin streams of smoke show how efficient the shape is. If the smoke curls, as on the Peugeot, the car will be hard to move through the air at speed. The Jaguar still shows these smoke curls, or turbulence. Today's Lexus saloon disturbs the air much less.

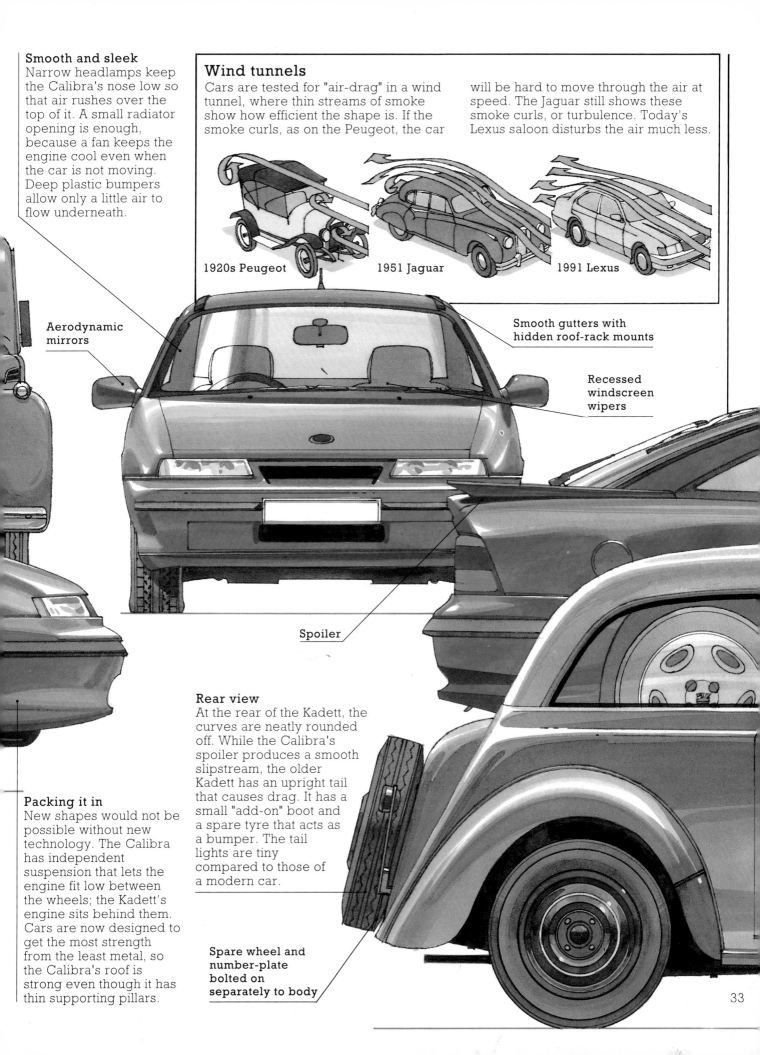

1920s Peugeot   1951 Jaguar   1991 Lexus

Aerodynamic mirrors

Smooth gutters with hidden roof-rack mounts

Recessed windscreen wipers

Spoiler

Rear view

At the rear of the Kadett, the curves are neatly rounded off. While the Calibra's spoiler produces a smooth slipstream, the older Kadett has an upright tail that causes drag. It has a small "add-on" boot and a spare tyre that acts as a bumper. The tail lights are tiny compared to those of a modern car.

Packing it in

New shapes would not be possible without new technology. The Calibra has independent suspension that lets the engine fit low between the wheels; the Kadett's engine sits behind them. Cars are now designed to get the most strength from the least metal, so the Calibra's roof is strong even though it has thin supporting pillars.

Spare wheel and number-plate bolted on separately to body

BODYWORK

"Bodywork" is an old-fashioned term dating back to the days when all cars had a bodyshell attached to a chassis. Manufacturers could offer several body styles for the same car, and change them quickly. Some firms, such as Rolls-Royce, sold only chassis. Others specialized in producing elaborate and beautiful car bodies. These firms were known as coachworks, because many of them had begun by building horse-drawn coaches.

Today, most modern cars do not have a separate chassis and body. Instead they have all-in-one steel bodies. This method of construction produces strong, light structures that are ideal for assembly by robots. Modern cars are also cheaper to build, but once the car is in production, even a small change to the design can cost millions of pounds. A few specialist car manufacturers still build cars with chassis.

Pre-planned panels
Most cars are built of steel panels welded together. They must fit together exactly, so every detail must be thought out beforehand. Some panels, such as the wings and bonnet, can be replaced after an accident. After a big crash, a garage may remove all the parts and fit them into a new shell.

On the level
Cars need suspension to ride smoothly over bumps in the road and to keep the tyres on the ground at all times. All types of suspension need a damper, or shock absorber, to stop the wheel from continuing to bounce after a bump. Independent suspension allows one side of the car to roll over a bump without affecting the other side, giving better road handling and a smoother ride than the old beam-axle suspension. However, some four-wheel drive vehicles still use beam axles because they are simple and sturdy.

Beam axle

Independent suspension

Under the skin
The body of a modern car cannot be removed, unlike the body of a Model T Ford (pages 14-15). Today's bodyshells are assembled from many different panels that do not require a separate chassis. But if the upper panels of a Nissan Sunny could be taken apart, you would see something like this. Joined together, the lower panels make up what is known as the floorpan.

Windscreens are made of tough, laminated glass

Up front
The engine bay is the most complex section of the bodyshell. It needs to be strong, to carry the engine and front suspension. It also has to be designed to fold up in an accident (pages 28-29). Cooling air must be able to get through the radiator grille easily. And there must be room for a mechanic to work on the engine's many components.

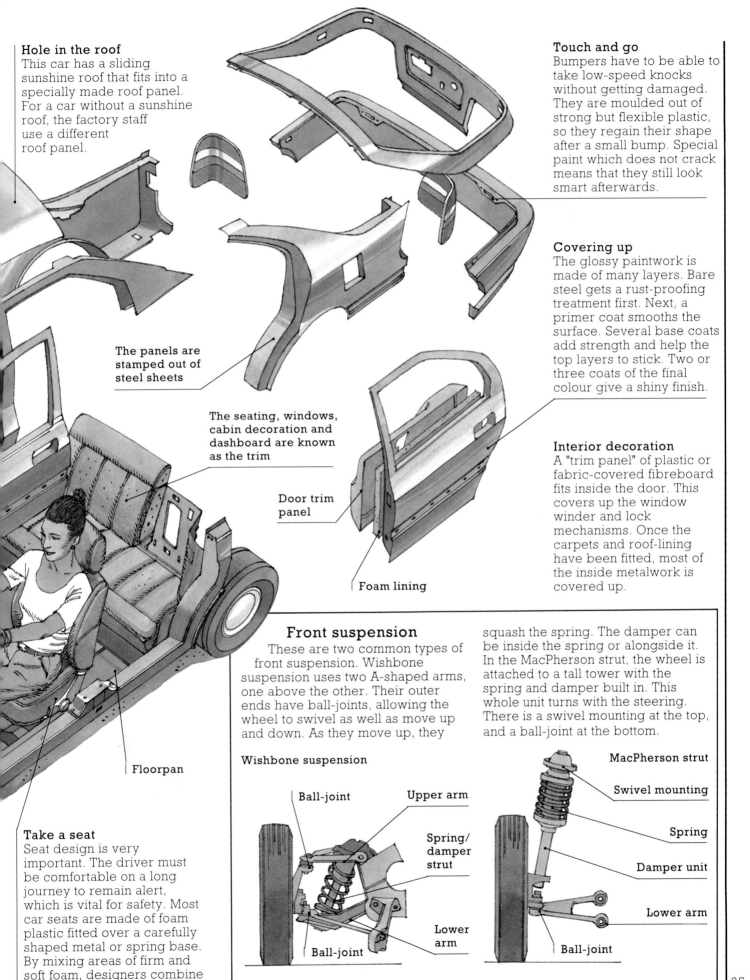

Hole in the roof
This car has a sliding sunshine roof that fits into a specially made roof panel. For a car without a sunshine roof, the factory staff use a different roof panel.

Touch and go
Bumpers have to be able to take low-speed knocks without getting damaged. They are moulded out of strong but flexible plastic, so they regain their shape after a small bump. Special paint which does not crack means that they still look smart afterwards.

The panels are stamped out of steel sheets

Covering up
The glossy paintwork is made of many layers. Bare steel gets a rust-proofing treatment first. Next, a primer coat smooths the surface. Several base coats add strength and help the top layers to stick. Two or three coats of the final colour give a shiny finish.

The seating, windows, cabin decoration and dashboard are known as the trim

Door trim panel

Interior decoration
A "trim panel" of plastic or fabric-covered fibreboard fits inside the door. This covers up the window winder and lock mechanisms. Once the carpets and roof-lining have been fitted, most of the inside metalwork is covered up.

Foam lining

Floorpan

Take a seat
Seat design is very important. The driver must be comfortable on a long journey to remain alert, which is vital for safety. Most car seats are made of foam plastic fitted over a carefully shaped metal or spring base. By mixing areas of firm and soft foam, designers combine comfort with good support.

Front suspension
These are two common types of front suspension. Wishbone suspension uses two A-shaped arms, one above the other. Their outer ends have ball-joints, allowing the wheel to swivel as well as move up and down. As they move up, they squash the spring. The damper can be inside the spring or alongside it. In the MacPherson strut, the wheel is attached to a tall tower with the spring and damper built in. This whole unit turns with the steering. There is a swivel mounting at the top, and a ball-joint at the bottom.

Wishbone suspension

Ball-joint

Upper arm

Spring/ damper strut

Lower arm

Ball-joint

MacPherson strut

Swivel mounting

Spring

Damper unit

Lower arm

Ball-joint

CARS FOR LEISURE

We are now so used to motoring that we often forget that it was once exciting and unusual. The Sunday drive was a weekly pleasure, whether going for a picnic or heading out for a day at the beach. Today, roads are often crowded and hold-ups are frequent. Yet driving remains a convenient way to travel. Five people can travel together, with their luggage in the boot. It saves carrying shopping on a bus or train, though people can become lazy, relying on cars even for short trips. Cars also help us follow our leisure and sporting interests. The whole family can go touring in the countryside. Cyclists can get out of town quickly with their bikes on the roof. Skiers and fishermen can head for the hills and rivers each weekend. The problem comes when everyone uses the same road to come home on Sunday night!

Outdoor elegance
In the 1920s, when cars were still a novelty, simply going for a drive was a pleasure in itself. Cars gave some families their first chance to get out into the countryside. Picnics became very fashionable, and wealthy folk carried elaborate picnic sets that included fine china and silver cutlery.

Roaming abroad
Holiday excitement fills the car as a family queues up to board a ferry. Having a car makes it easy to take along everything that is needed for a perfect holiday. There are trailers and caravans, bicycles and boats - plus a fortnight's luggage for everyone. The family car has to work hard on holiday!

Tagging on behind
A car can move more weight by towing a trailer. This water-ski enthusiast has a speedboat attached to the back of the car. Box-trailers can give an ordinary car the luggage space of a van. Riders use horse-boxes to transport their animals.

Room on top
When there is too much luggage to fit into the boot, a roof-rack provides more carrying space. The first roof-racks added extra air-drag (page 33), but this modern, fibreglass luggage box has a more streamlined shape.

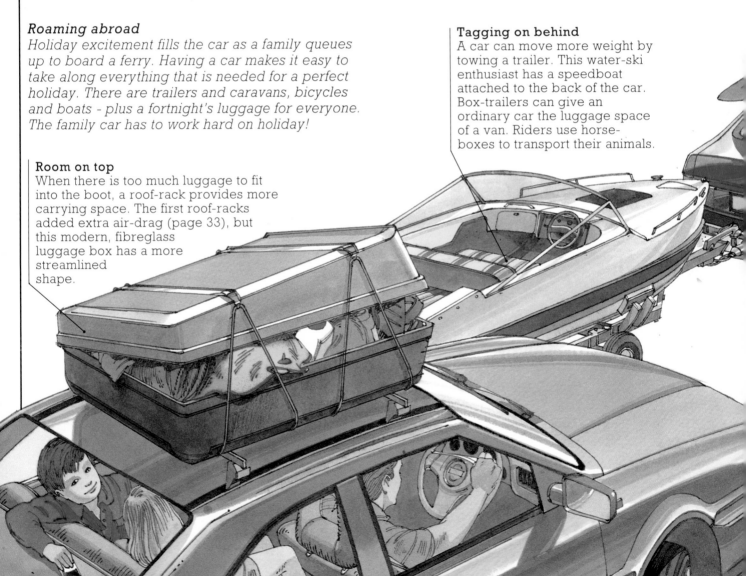

Roll-on, roll-off

Giant "roll-on, roll-off" ferries carry hundreds of cars and lorries on several decks. Vehicles drive in through huge bow (front) doors and out at the stern (rear). On busy waterways, such as the English Channel, they run day and night without stopping.

Home from home

Caravans are "mobile homes" that you can take on holiday. They range from two-berth caravans, light enough for a Mini to pull, to giant-size versions. The kitchens and beds fold away to save space.

Surfboards are easily carried on a roof-rack

Wheels on the roof

Some things are too bulky to fit inside the car. With a rack, the driver can mount them securely on the roof. This rack can carry two full-size bicycles. Skis, ladders and fishing rods all have their own special fittings. Even small boats can be carried on the roof.

Load-lugging

In the early days, motorists simply strapped their luggage on to the back of the car. Some manufacturers added a lockable trunk, and later a built-in locker. By the 1950s proper boots had been introduced, with the spare tyre tucked underneath. Today's hatchback is nearly as roomy as an estate car.

This 1934 Delage from France has a small boot with a two-piece lid

The boot of this 1954 Riley has a big lid with the spare tyre under the floor

Fiat's tiny Panda hatchback can swallow large objects

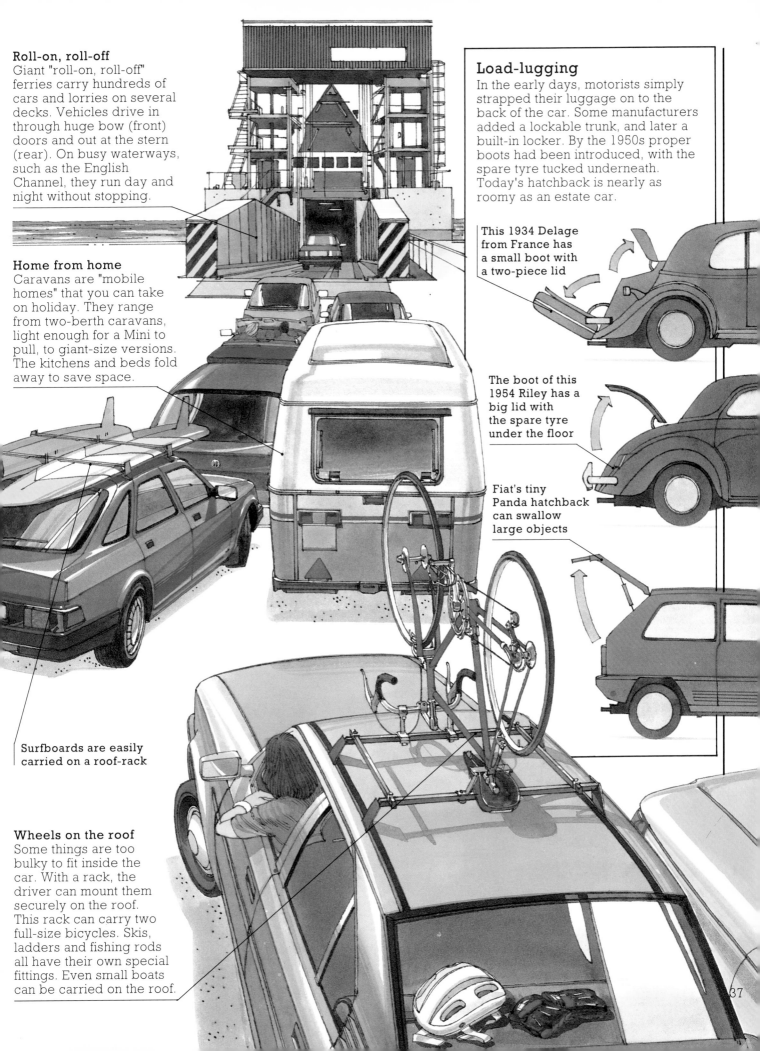

BREAKDOWN

Cars today are very reliable considering the huge distances they cover. In the early 1900s everyone carried a good tool kit because they expected problems; now most people pack nothing except a tyre spanner and jack for punctures. Cars are so complex that few drivers could cope with any other problem, so many join a breakdown club. This has hundreds of repair vans, all connected by radio. A computer keeps track of where they are, and the control centre stays open night and day. Once a motorist rings up and tells them their problem, they will call up the nearest patrol.

Holiday hold-up
While the holiday traffic flows along the motorway, a family wait for the repairman to mend their car. Soon, he should get the car going. If not he will load the car on a trailer and take them to their destination. Or he may do a temporary "get you home" repair, which must be done properly later.

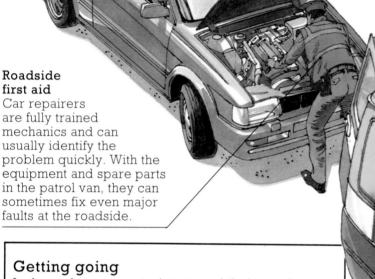

Roadside first aid
Car repairers are fully trained mechanics and can usually identify the problem quickly. With the equipment and spare parts in the patrol van, they can sometimes fix even major faults at the roadside.

Tools and spares are securely fixed in racks

Bright flashing lights to warn other drivers

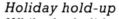

Getting going

In the early years motorists started their cars by turning a handle, but this was hard work. By the 1930s electric starters were common. However, for many years they were not reliable, so manufacturers fitted a starting handle for emergencies. Today's cars have no handle, so a flat battery means using jump leads, which connect the car to a fresh battery, or a tow-start.

If the engine backfired, the driver risked being hit by the handle

Strong jack for lifting cars

Well stocked
The breakdown van is packed with tools, such as spanners, wrenches, a jack, a tyre pump, jump leads and a powerful torch. There are also spare parts, such as fanbelts and alternators (page 39). If the car repairers do not carry a certain part, they can order it by radio-telephone.

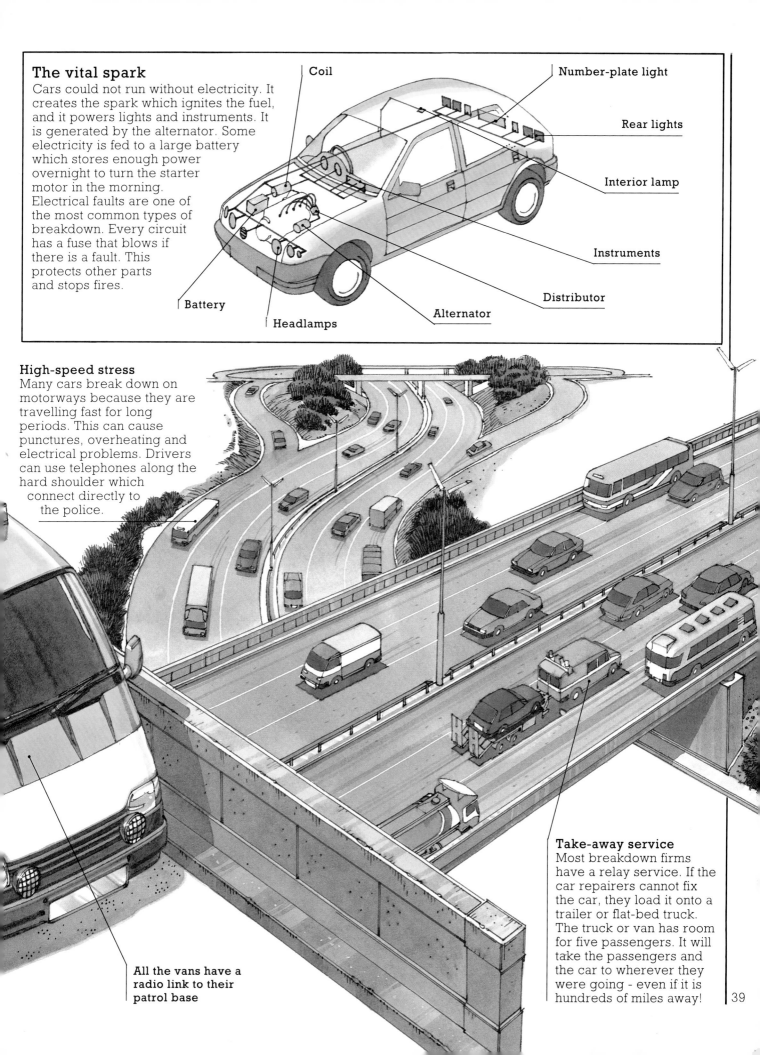

The vital spark

Cars could not run without electricity. It creates the spark which ignites the fuel, and it powers lights and instruments. It is generated by the alternator. Some electricity is fed to a large battery which stores enough power overnight to turn the starter motor in the morning. Electrical faults are one of the most common types of breakdown. Every circuit has a fuse that blows if there is a fault. This protects other parts and stops fires.

Coil

Number-plate light

Rear lights

Interior lamp

Instruments

Distributor

Battery

Headlamps

Alternator

High-speed stress

Many cars break down on motorways because they are travelling fast for long periods. This can cause punctures, overheating and electrical problems. Drivers can use telephones along the hard shoulder which connect directly to the police.

All the vans have a radio link to their patrol base

Take-away service

Most breakdown firms have a relay service. If the car repairers cannot fix the car, they load it onto a trailer or flat-bed truck. The truck or van has room for five passengers. It will take the passengers and the car to wherever they were going - even if it is hundreds of miles away!

AMAZING CARS

We see ordinary cars around us every day, but there are some truly astonishing cars that you will rarely see in your local high street. Some were designed for more than one purpose, such as the flying Aerocar, or the Amphicar, which drives on land and in water. The Aerocar was a failure, and cost more than buying an aeroplane and a car together. But the Amphicar was a success, and several hundred were sold. Today, they are both collectors' cars.

Another type is the show car. These expensive "one-offs" are displayed at motor shows to win publicity for the big car companies. They are hardly ever sold to the public, but they incorporate new ideas that may shape the cars of the future.

Amazing cars are also built to perform film stunts (pages 54-55). Others are produced for advertising. There have been cars disguised as beer bottles, houses and space rockets. But even the craziest and strangest cars need skill and imagination to make them perform well and look good.

Seaside surprises
Sunbathers stare as a motor-boat drives on to the beach and turns out to be a car as well. Overhead, the pilot of a small aeroplane is puzzled to see a giant orange trundling along the sea-front. He decides to investigate. He lands at a nearby airstrip, unclips the tail and wings, and drives his flying car back to the beach. It is certainly a day for surprises!

Detachable tail-section with "pusher" propeller

The Aerocar had a wingspan of 10.4m (34ft)

Fruit on the move
In the 1970s a firm that sold fruit built some "mobile oranges". They used a Mini engine and transmission mounted in a special short chassis, with a fibreglass "skin". Working lights and wipers meant that these motorized fruits could drive on the road. They were not fast, but they were good advertisements for the company.

Water wagon
The German Amphicar appeared in the early 1960s. It travelled at 12kph (7.5mph) on water and 120kph (75mph) on the road. Rubber seals in the doors kept water out. Its rear engine drove either the wheels or two small propellers under the tail. Afloat, the driver steered with the front wheels.

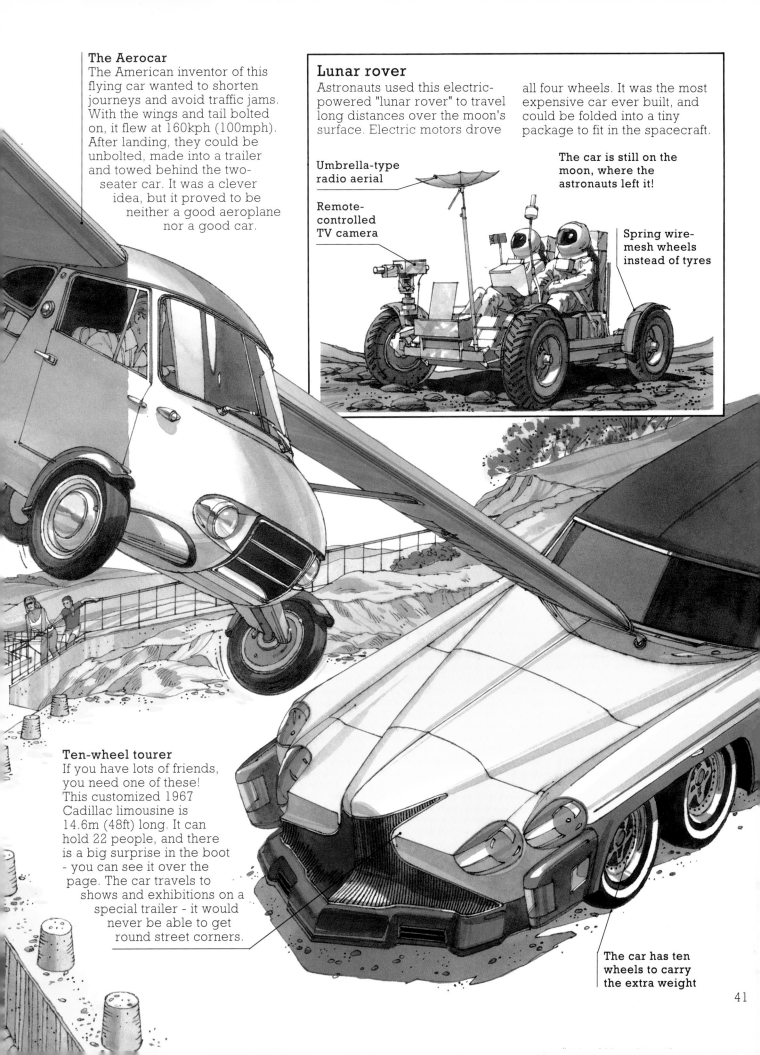

The Aerocar

The American inventor of this flying car wanted to shorten journeys and avoid traffic jams. With the wings and tail bolted on, it flew at 160kph (100mph). After landing, they could be unbolted, made into a trailer and towed behind the two-seater car. It was a clever idea, but it proved to be neither a good aeroplane nor a good car.

Lunar rover

Astronauts used this electric-powered "lunar rover" to travel long distances over the moon's surface. Electric motors drove all four wheels. It was the most expensive car ever built, and could be folded into a tiny package to fit in the spacecraft.

Umbrella-type radio aerial

Remote-controlled TV camera

The car is still on the moon, where the astronauts left it!

Spring wire-mesh wheels instead of tyres

Ten-wheel tourer

If you have lots of friends, you need one of these! This customized 1967 Cadillac limousine is 14.6m (48ft) long. It can hold 22 people, and there is a big surprise in the boot - you can see it over the page. The car travels to shows and exhibitions on a special trailer - it would never be able to get round street corners.

The car has ten wheels to carry the extra weight

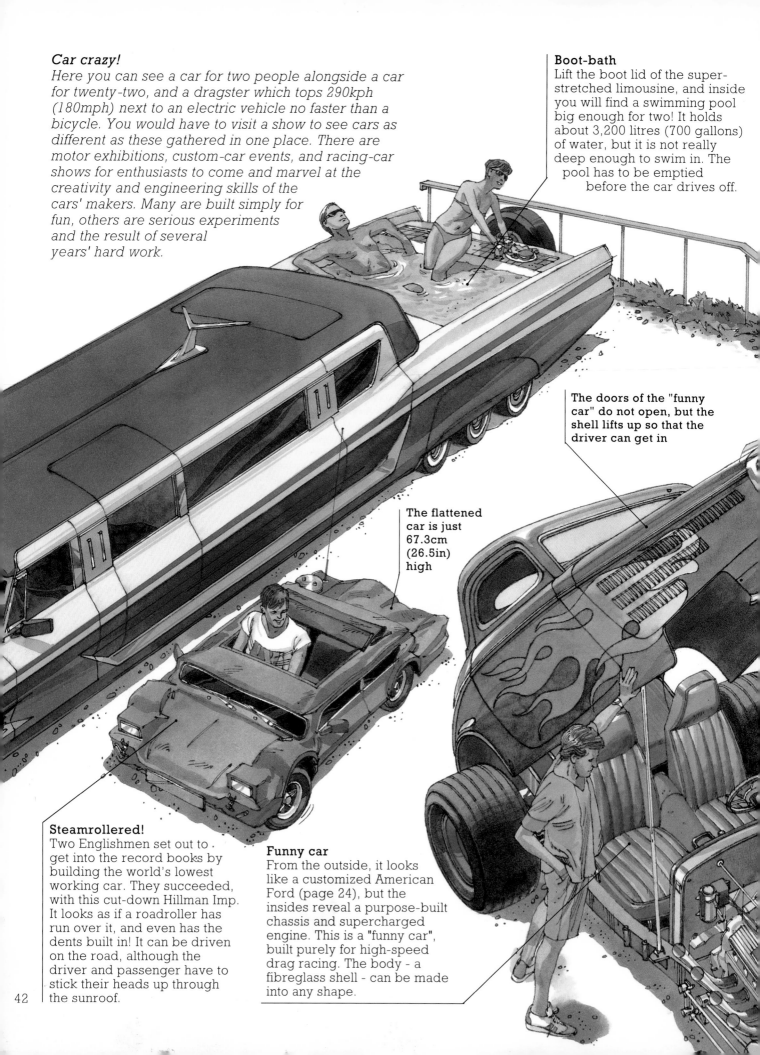

Car crazy!

Here you can see a car for two people alongside a car for twenty-two, and a dragster which tops 290kph (180mph) next to an electric vehicle no faster than a bicycle. You would have to visit a show to see cars as different as these gathered in one place. There are motor exhibitions, custom-car events, and racing-car shows for enthusiasts to come and marvel at the creativity and engineering skills of the cars' makers. Many are built simply for fun, others are serious experiments and the result of several years' hard work.

Boot-bath

Lift the boot lid of the super-stretched limousine, and inside you will find a swimming pool big enough for two! It holds about 3,200 litres (700 gallons) of water, but it is not really deep enough to swim in. The pool has to be emptied before the car drives off.

The doors of the "funny car" do not open, but the shell lifts up so that the driver can get in

The flattened car is just 67.3cm (26.5in) high

Steamrollered!

Two Englishmen set out to get into the record books by building the world's lowest working car. They succeeded, with this cut-down Hillman Imp. It looks as if a roadroller has run over it, and even has the dents built in! It can be driven on the road, although the driver and passenger have to stick their heads up through the sunroof.

Funny car

From the outside, it looks like a customized American Ford (page 24), but the insides reveal a purpose-built chassis and supercharged engine. This is a "funny car", built purely for high-speed drag racing. The body - a fibreglass shell - can be made into any shape.

Rolling thunder

Drag racing is one of the most spectacular motor sports. The aim is to sprint down a straight 400-m (440-yard) track as fast as possible from a standing start. Cars race in pairs, side-by-side, reaching 370kph (230mph), and need parachutes to slow down.

The engines are so powerful that they sometimes lift the skinny front wheels high into the air

Massive rear tyres give excellent grip

Huge supercharged engines

Two in one

Mini-vans are popular, but they use up a lot of petrol when driving around town. So Chrysler designed this two-in-one mini-van, called Voyager III, as a show car. When the two halves are joined, it carries eight people. The front section unclips to become a three-seater city car. It has a small engine in the front and a large engine in the rear, which adds power when the car becomes a mini-van.

Battery trike

In 1984 a British inventor, Sir Clive Sinclair, produced this three-wheeled electric moped. Although it was cheap to run, the Sinclair C5 only went for 32km (20 miles) on its battery. It had pedals too, but pedalling was hard work. Sinclair hoped to improve on his idea, but the C5 did not prove popular.

The C5 was just 1.7m (5ft 8in) long

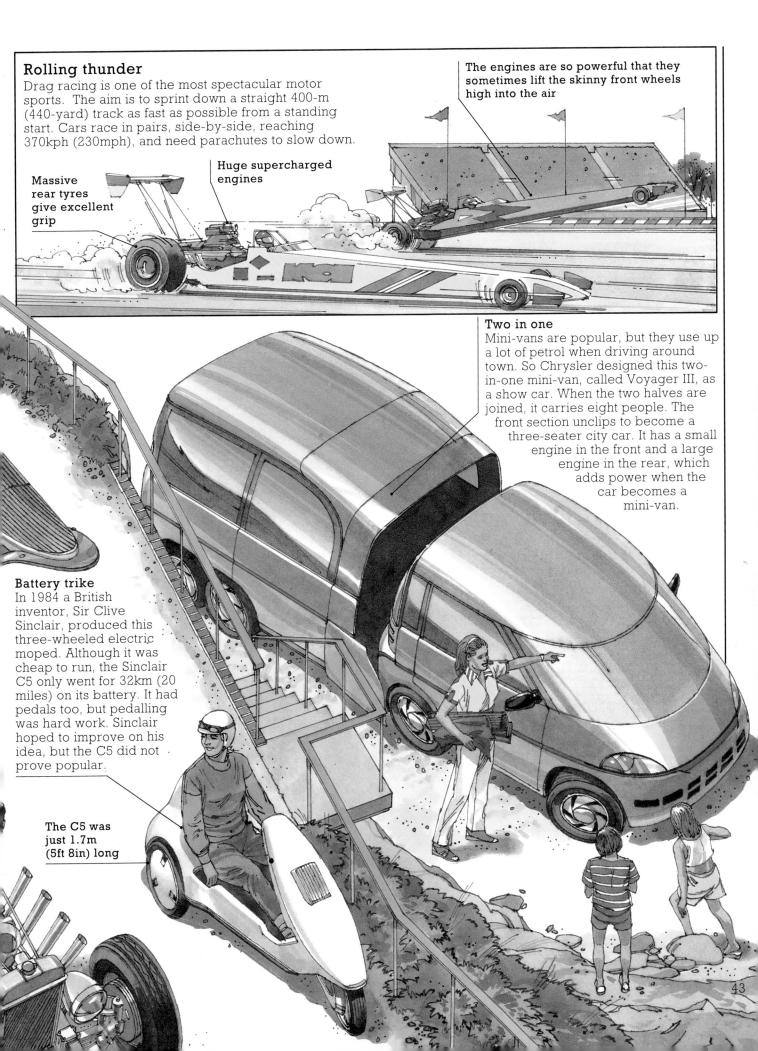

ROUGH RIDING

Rallying is a fast and tough sport. It is very different to racing, where all the cars compete on the track at the same time. Rally cars all follow the same route, one after another. The cars may drive along mountain tracks, forest roads, or public roads that have been closed by the police. The route is split into sections called "stages", with time-control points between them. Important rallies last for several days and there can be up to 40 stages, with 80 or 90 controls. The cars are based on saloon cars, but are converted so they are much faster, noisier and stronger. They have front seats, but no rear seats or carpets. Beside the driver sits the co-driver, who uses maps and special instructions called pace-notes to tell the driver where to go and how fast to drive. Rallies run in winter and summer, from snowy Scandinavia down to the baking heat of East Africa.

Keeping time
Marshalls wait at every control to mark each co-driver's time-card with the time the car arrived. This will show whether the car reached all the controls and the time taken overall.

Fast and furious
Lights ablaze, a Ford Escort Cosworth hurtles off into the dark forest, bouncing and sliding on the loose track. While the driver forges ahead, using great skill and expert reflexes, the co-driver reads out his pace-notes to warn of sharp bends or big bumps.

Radio aerial

Twice the grip
Rally cars look like ordinary saloon cars but they are fitted with turbocharged engines, special tyres for firm grip and powerful brakes. Top rally cars have four-wheel drive (page 49), which provides better grip on loose roads.

4

Strong and safe

The rally team have to make their car as tough and as safe as possible. They build in a steel roll-cage which forms a strong framework around the crew, protecting them if the car overturns or crashes. They also fit the car with a fire-proof fuel tank, a fire extinguisher and very strong suspension. The crew sit in high-sided seats, wearing fireproof overalls, gloves and shoes that can make them hot and uncomfortable when rallying in a warm country.

The roll-cage is bolted inside the body of the car

Lightweight "bucket" seats provide extra support

Fireproof overalls

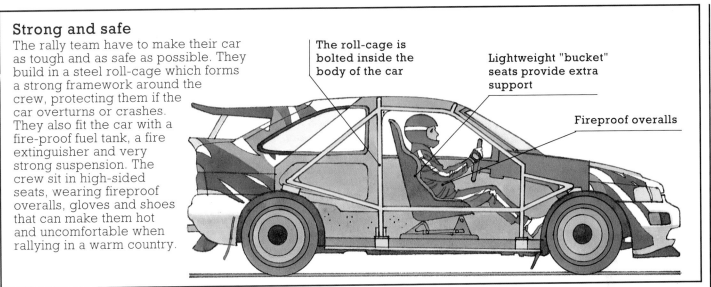

Over and out

Top teams have two-way radios in each car and in the mechanics' vans. If the car should break down, the co-driver radios ahead for help. The mechanics can only work on the car at certain places, so they need to know which spare parts to have ready in time for the car's arrival.

In touch

The crew must always wear safety helmets. They have built-in microphones and headphones, which means that the driver can hear the co-driver's instructions even though it is very noisy inside the car.

Anti-dazzle

When travelling at night on a rally stage a driver can use bright lights safely. Between stages, the cars travel on ordinary roads, so the drivers dip their headlamps on meeting oncoming vehicles. The light is less bright and points lower down. Lamps giving a broad fan of light are used in fog.

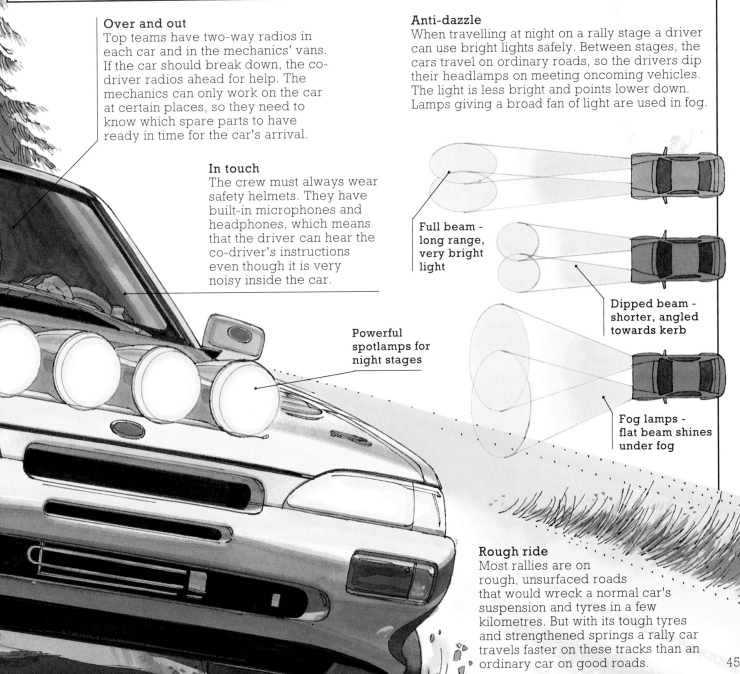

Full beam - long range, very bright light

Dipped beam - shorter, angled towards kerb

Fog lamps - flat beam shines under fog

Powerful spotlamps for night stages

Rough ride

Most rallies are on rough, unsurfaced roads that would wreck a normal car's suspension and tyres in a few kilometres. But with its tough tyres and strengthened springs a rally car travels faster on these tracks than an ordinary car on good roads.

45

SMALL CARS

Many people prefer small cars to large ones. They are easy to drive and to park, and often they are cheaper to buy and to run. In the 1920s and 1930s, when motoring was an expensive hobby, inventors tried to make tiny, simple cars which were very cheap. They hoped everyone could buy one. But they were often slow, unsafe and uncomfortable. Then companies began to make small, cheap cars that would carry two adults and two children. Britain's Austin Seven and the Italian Fiat Topolino were very successful examples. When ordinary people became used to motoring, they wanted more room. So along came cars like the German Volkswagen and the British Morris Minor. They were not very small, but they were simple. The British Mini was the first real four-seater small car.

Parking pressures

Every year more cars fight for parking spaces on crowded city streets. Small nippy cars that can turn tight corners are easy to park, and use less fuel in heavy traffic. Today, car manufacturers build compact models that can easily carry four passengers, but are still not too large for the town.

Minor classic

Four people and their luggage could ride comfortably in the Morris Minor 1000. Very popular in the 1950s and 1960s, it had a "poached egg" shape, was easy to drive and had a simple engine. It coped with rough tracks as well as good roads, and was easy to repair.

Italian design

In the 1950s, the two-seater Isetta, with its huge front door, set a trend for "bubble cars". Its two rear wheels were set so close together that it looked like a three-wheeler. It was little longer than a bicycle, and could park in tiny spaces.

Four-seater motorbike

Three-wheelers are easy to drive and cheap to run. In Britain you only need a motorbike licence to drive one. The British firm Reliant has been building three-wheelers since 1935 and this Reliant Rialto was first made in 1982. Today, they have 750cc engines and fibreglass bodies, with a single wheel at the front. There is just enough room for four people inside. Reliant also make sports cars and London taxis.

Beetlemania

More Volkswagen Beetles have been made than any other car. It was designed over 50 years ago to be sturdy and cheap to run. *Volkswagen* means "people's car" and the car gave many German families their first chance to go motoring. It became one of the world's best-loved cars.

Mini bus-load

The Mini is famous for many things. Because it is so small, people compete to cram as many on board as possible. They can sit on the roof and hang out of the windows, but no one must touch the ground. Despite its size, the record is 46 people, set by students in Australia.

The car must be driven 5m (16ft 4in) to qualify for the record

Roll-back roof

Italians have always liked "baby" cars. The neat-looking Fiat 500 used a tiny, air-cooled, two-cylinder engine at the rear. It was cheap to buy and run, and easy to park, though it could not carry four adults. Its roll-back canvas top made it fun to drive in hot weather. You can still see many driving around, though Fiat stopped making them in 1973.

A revolution

At last - an economy car which took four people and their luggage. The 1959 Morris Mini turned the engine sideways and had tiny wheels and clever rubber suspension to leave most of the space inside for the passengers. Now almost every small car has a similar design.

Japanese flair

Today's small cars are getting bigger - on the inside. Mazda's 121 is a bit longer than a Mini, but has much more passenger room. Like many new designs it is very tall, with four doors, giving good space in the back.

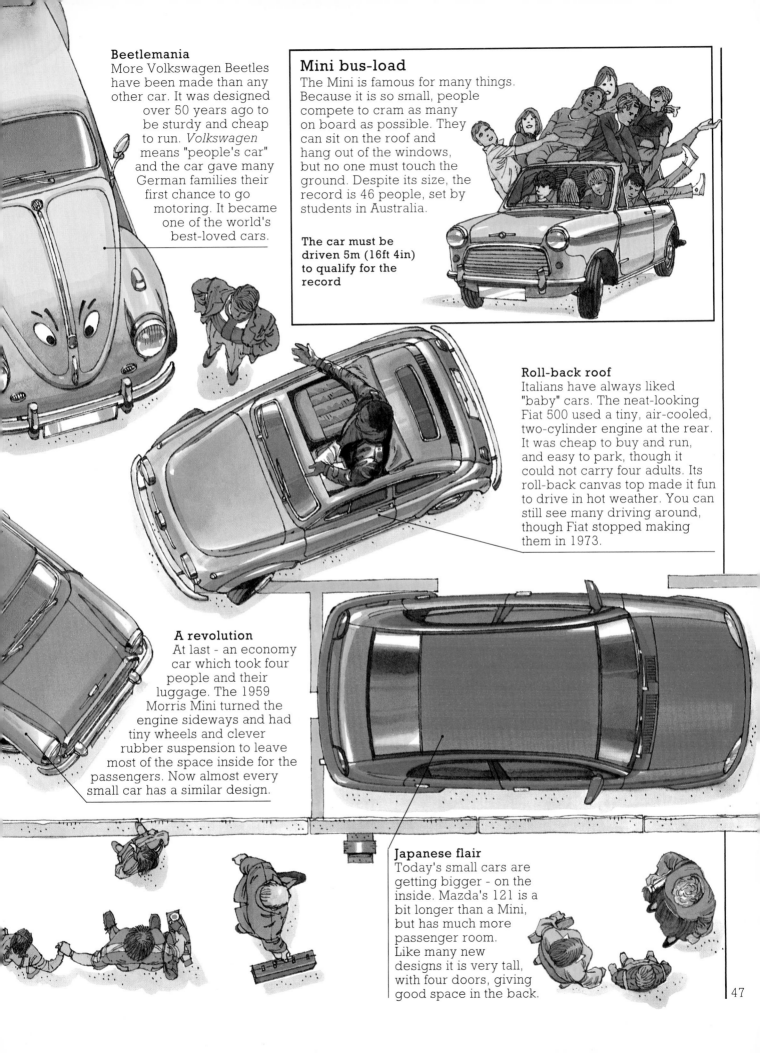

OFF THE ROAD

Ordinary cars can only drive over fairly smooth surfaces. They would soon get stuck if they tried to leave the road. But some people need to travel over rough country. Farmers and firefighters, for example, need special "off-road" vehicles for their jobs. These cars sit high off the ground to avoid hitting rocks, and have strong tyres with knobbly treads to grip in mud and dust. Most of them use all four wheels to pull themselves along (four-wheel drive) so that they can keep going when the ground is slippery. Powerful engines and low gears help them to climb steep hills, while easily broken parts, such as the exhaust, are tucked out of the way. Countries with poor roads rely on these vehicles for transport. The first light, four-wheel drive off-road car was the Jeep, built for the United States army in the Second World War (1939-1945).

Off-roaders

Whether it is wildlife spotting, racing over sand dunes or climbing snowy tracks, off-road cars can tackle many tasks. Some are used for pleasure, such as going camping in the bush. Other off-roaders save lives. In heavy snow they may be the only way a doctor can reach a sick patient.

World-wide work-horse

British Land-Rovers can act as trucks, tow-cars and ambulances. They can drive through 90-120cm (3-4ft) of water without stopping. This Safari model can carry up to 12 people. Its roof opens, allowing passengers to watch animals on the African plains.

Jeep

Although the body and engine have changed, the Jeep still has the same basic layout as it did over 50 years ago. The short nose and tail help it climb steep banks. Once meant as a work machine, the Jeep is now a popular leisure vehicle.

A roll-bar is added in case the vehicle overturns

Desert racer
Buggies can go racing on sand and mud. They are single-seaters, and have simple, light, steel frames with the engine in the back (usually a Volkswagen, but sometimes a more powerful Porsche). Only the rear wheels are driven, and they have fat tyres to run on sand. The front is so light it only needs thin tyres.

The roll-cage is part of the car frame

The front suspension needs tough dampers to absorb high-speed shocks when bouncing over rough ground

Narrow front wheels

Wide rear tyres with chunky tread

Double drive
In four-wheel drive vehicles, the drive is split behind the gearbox so that some goes to the front and some to the rear. This is done by a differential (page 31). The front propeller shaft is moved to the side of the engine and driven by a transfer box. The front and rear propeller shafts both drive their axles through differentials, as normal.

Front propeller shaft

Rear propeller shaft

Rear differential

Gearbox

Transfer box and centre differential

Front differential

Dual purpose
Early off-road vehicles were bare and simple, but today some are like luxury cars. This German Mercedes G-wagen is not only good on rough ground, but also fast and comfortable on ordinary roads.

FORMULA ONE

Motor racing is one of the world's most popular and exciting sports. Huge television audiences watch their racing heroes compete at breathtaking speeds - around 320kph (200mph) - for the honour of winning a Formula One race, the highest class in racing. It costs millions of pounds to build and run a Formula One car. Teams rely on sponsorship from big international companies, which pay huge sums to advertise their names on the cars. There is great rivalry between the teams, and they constantly try to improve their cars so that they have the edge over the others in a race. These sleek, low cars are built of lightweight materials to maximize their speed. Racing is very tough on the cars - especially the engines - and they usually have to be rebuilt completely after each race.

Grand Prix pit-stop

As the Formula One cars fight it out on the track, a Williams-Honda and a Ferrari pull into the pits. Mechanics leap into action with jacks and power tools to fit new tyres. They must take just a few seconds or their car may fall behind and lose the race.

Quick turnaround
If this Ferrari driver feels his tyres are wearing down, he radios his pit so that the mechanics are ready when he pulls in. They jack the car up, loosen the wheelnuts, change the tyres and tighten the nuts again.

The first circuit
Brooklands was built in 1907 and was the first car-racing track in the world. It was built in England, where racing on public roads was not permitted, unlike other countries where cars raced on blocked-off roads. At Brooklands, cars could reach very high speeds on the steep concrete banking. The fastest car ever around the track used an aeroplane engine, and lapped at 237kph (147mph). The track closed in 1939, but part of the banking remains as a museum.

Fast cars drove along the top of the banking, while slower cars stayed lower down

Push-start
According to race rules, a car must move under its own power. Pushing is only allowed during practice. If a car's engine stops in a race, the driver must restart it or be disqualified. If the car goes off the track and gets stuck, no one is allowed to help.

Weaving a trail

Cars may weave to the left and right before the start of a race. This warms the tyres so that they grip the track well as the car accelerates away from a standstill. A kind of "electric blanket" keeps tyres warm at pit-stops.

Tyres are made of soft rubber which gives the best grip when hot

The cars weave snake-like paths as they drive up to the start

A good team can change a car's tyres in less than eight seconds

Mechanics use sign-boards to tell drivers what position they are in

Marshalling help

This marshal has an extinguisher and wears a flameproof suit and helmet. He will help the driver if a car catches fire. There are marshals all around the circuit, and they can be at the scene of a crash in just a few seconds. They also remove debris from the track and stop spectators crossing the barriers.

Slicks and wets

Racing cars have special tyres that enable them to go around corners at amazing speeds. The fastest cars, like this Williams-Honda, run on "slick" tyres. These smooth tyres have no tread, and in dry weather they stick to the track like glue. If it rains during a race, the drivers will change to "wet" tyres, which have grooves, to give them a better grip on the watery track.

Mid-mounted engine

Fuel tank

Roll-over hoop

Side-mounted radiators

Air scoops to cool brakes

51

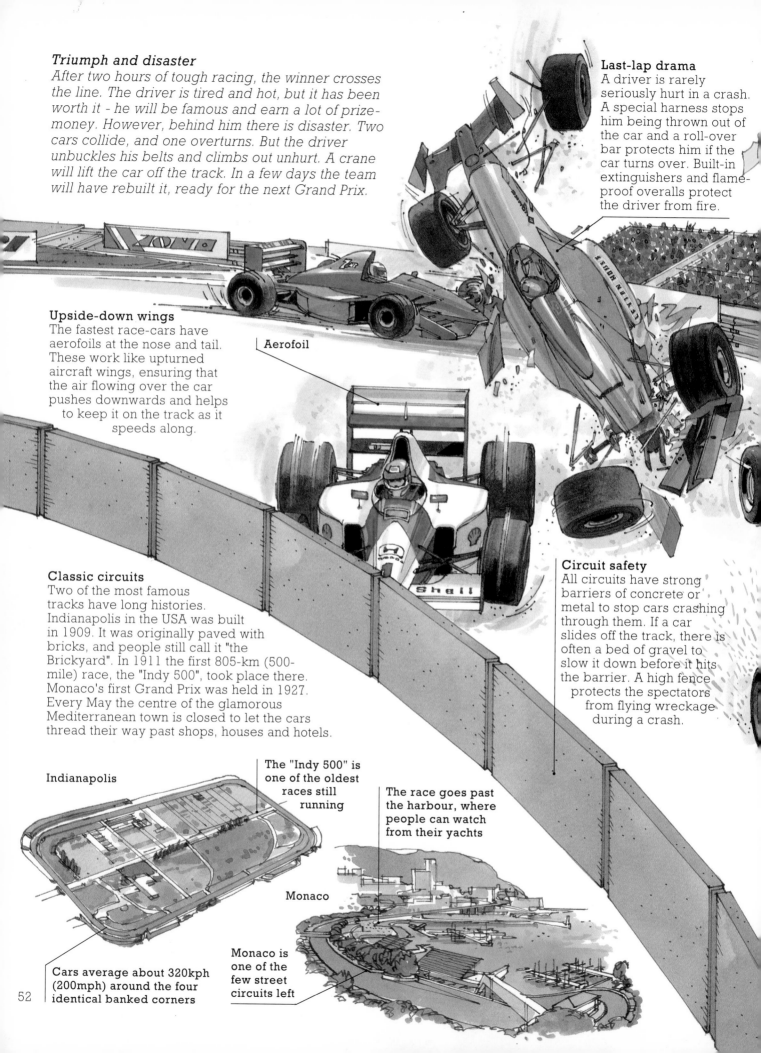

Triumph and disaster

After two hours of tough racing, the winner crosses the line. The driver is tired and hot, but it has been worth it - he will be famous and earn a lot of prize-money. However, behind him there is disaster. Two cars collide, and one overturns. But the driver unbuckles his belts and climbs out unhurt. A crane will lift the car off the track. In a few days the team will have rebuilt it, ready for the next Grand Prix.

Last-lap drama

A driver is rarely seriously hurt in a crash. A special harness stops him being thrown out of the car and a roll-over bar protects him if the car turns over. Built-in extinguishers and flame-proof overalls protect the driver from fire.

Upside-down wings

The fastest race-cars have aerofoils at the nose and tail. These work like upturned aircraft wings, ensuring that the air flowing over the car pushes downwards and helps to keep it on the track as it speeds along.

Aerofoil

Classic circuits

Two of the most famous tracks have long histories. Indianapolis in the USA was built in 1909. It was originally paved with bricks, and people still call it "the Brickyard". In 1911 the first 805-km (500-mile) race, the "Indy 500", took place there. Monaco's first Grand Prix was held in 1927. Every May the centre of the glamorous Mediterranean town is closed to let the cars thread their way past shops, houses and hotels.

Circuit safety

All circuits have strong barriers of concrete or metal to stop cars crashing through them. If a car slides off the track, there is often a bed of gravel to slow it down before it hits the barrier. A high fence protects the spectators from flying wreckage during a crash.

Indianapolis

The "Indy 500" is one of the oldest races still running

The race goes past the harbour, where people can watch from their yachts

Monaco

Cars average about 320kph (200mph) around the four identical banked corners

Monaco is one of the few street circuits left

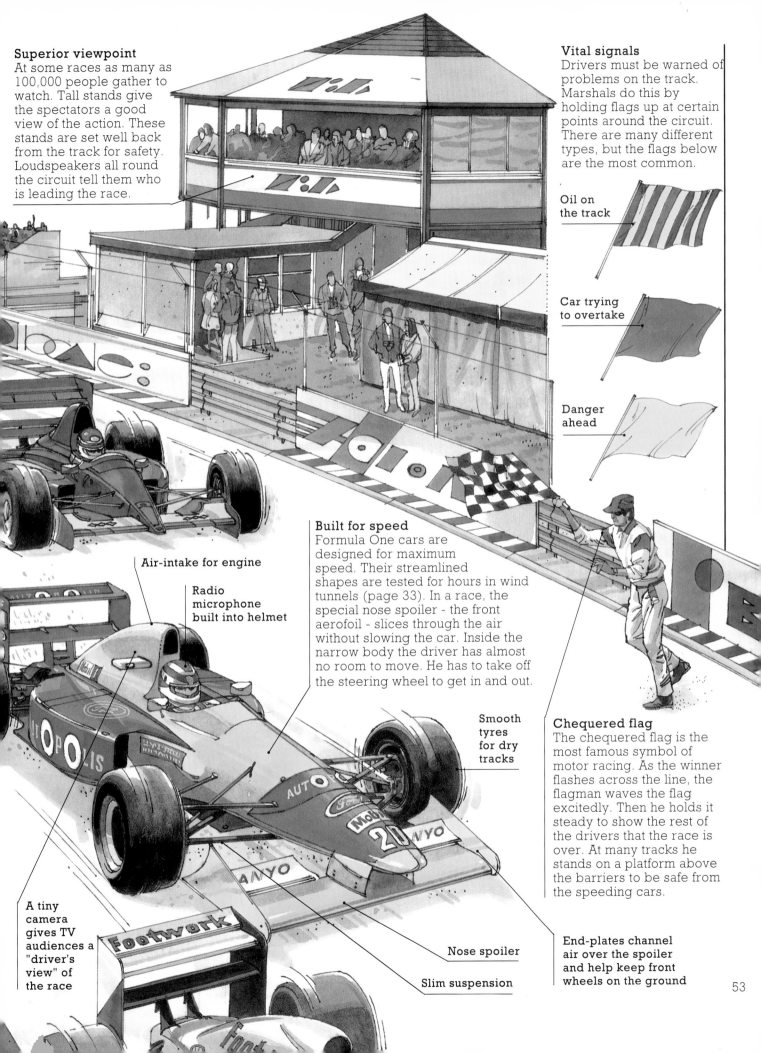

Superior viewpoint
At some races as many as 100,000 people gather to watch. Tall stands give the spectators a good view of the action. These stands are set well back from the track for safety. Loudspeakers all round the circuit tell them who is leading the race.

Vital signals
Drivers must be warned of problems on the track. Marshals do this by holding flags up at certain points around the circuit. There are many different types, but the flags below are the most common.

Oil on the track

Car trying to overtake

Danger ahead

Built for speed
Formula One cars are designed for maximum speed. Their streamlined shapes are tested for hours in wind tunnels (page 33). In a race, the special nose spoiler - the front aerofoil - slices through the air without slowing the car. Inside the narrow body the driver has almost no room to move. He has to take off the steering wheel to get in and out.

Chequered flag
The chequered flag is the most famous symbol of motor racing. As the winner flashes across the line, the flagman waves the flag excitedly. Then he holds it steady to show the rest of the drivers that the race is over. At many tracks he stands on a platform above the barriers to be safe from the speeding cars.

Air-intake for engine

Radio microphone built into helmet

A tiny camera gives TV audiences a "driver's view" of the race

Smooth tyres for dry tracks

Nose spoiler

Slim suspension

End-plates channel air over the spoiler and help keep front wheels on the ground

53

CARS ON FILM

Cars have been stars as long as movies have been made. From the crazy accidents of Laurel and Hardy to the dramatic stunts of James Bond, filmmakers have used cars for a wide variety of sensational scenes. Remote-controlled detonators can set off explosions or puncture a tyre. Petrol bombs can blow a car up after it has fallen down a cliff. Some cars "drive themselves", using someone hidden inside. Together, experts in "special effects" and experienced stunt performers will work out every detail beforehand. But in the end it is up to the skill of the driver to get it right when the cameras roll. Stunt drivers are used to crashing cars and they know how to make it look good. They must wear protective clothing, a harness and a crash helmet. They sometimes put "fire gel" on their flameproof clothing to make it look as if they are on fire. There is always a risk though, and most stunt performers have scars to prove it.

Movie mayhem

Today's action movies are often packed with spectacular scenes of cars crashing, flying through the air, exploding, and tumbling down cliffs. These dramatic shots last only minutes, or even seconds, but they take days to shoot and much longer to plan. While studio scenes can be shot and reshot until they are perfect, action stunts need to be right first time.

High jump

Car jumps are always spectacular. Using a big ramp, cars can jump roads, railways, or even rivers. Stunt experts can work out where the car will land from the height of the ramp and the speed of the car. Sometimes the suspension is toughened up so the car can keep going after the jump. More often the car breaks up and the crew tow it off the set. Cameras then film a similar car driving away and the film is edited, or joined, so that it looks like one smooth jump. To make a car turn over, the driver roars towards an angled ramp (1). As the car hits it, it begins to roll over (2). It twists into the air, and lands on its roof (3).

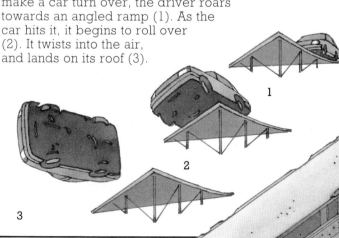

Bang!

A Porsche collides with some oil barrels and explodes - right in front of the cameras. An explosives expert uses a radio detonator to set off the charge when the car reaches exactly the right place. Despite the bright flash, it is a small explosion.

Inside this flying Mercedes is a roll-cage that forms a strong frame within the car

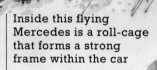

Outside inside

It is always good weather inside the studio, so many driving shots are filmed there. The actors sit in a car with no wheels, in front of a blue background. Electric fans blow their hair around to give a wind effect. A special rocking base makes this Maserati bounce as if it were moving. After shooting, a separate film of a road is added in the background. This only shows up on the blue background panel, not on the car or the actors.

The two separate films are combined on screen

Harmless flames

Although it is blazing brightly, this car may survive the fire and go through it again. Special fire gel is smeared over the car, producing vapour or gas that burns just above the surface of the bodywork. It scorches the paint, but it will not set the body alight.

Dummy drop

This Lamborghini is about to plunge into the valley and crash. The car is "fired" at the bridge by an air-cannon, or huge air-gun. Often, expensive parts like the engine are taken out first. Sometimes a fibreglass copy of the car is made. The bullet holes can be painted on.

On the road

For action on the move, a camera on a sturdy tripod films the actors as they stage a fight on the bonnet of this Aston Martin. Microphones inside the car pick up what they are saying. They can drive the car - slowly - wherever they want. There is no need for special background effects.

RECORD BREAKERS

From the moment the first Benz put-putted along the street, designers have competed to build the fastest car. The first world speed record for automobiles was recorded in 1898 when a Frenchman, Count Chasseloup-Laubat, touched 63.14kph (39.24mph) in his electric *Jeantaud* car. The land speed record became a tempting prize for daring and determined drivers. At first, record breakers used roads or race-tracks, then smooth beaches. Today, the cars run on salt lakes or deserts; the ground must be very smooth, as even a tiny bump can cause an upset. They need a straight course about 21km (13 miles) long: 10km (6 miles) to speed up, a timed run of 1.6km (1 mile) and 10km (6 miles) to slow down. The car is timed in both directions to cancel out any help from the wind. It must make its return run within one hour.

Flying on the ground

Record-breaking cars are always striking, and often beautiful. Most have used piston or jet aircraft engines to supply the tremendous power they require. Streamlined to slip through the air, they have tail fins like fighter planes to help the driver keep the car running straight. Most of these cars will only ever travel a few kilometres in their lives.

A brake parachute pops out to slow the car down after its run

Torpedo on wheels

Camille Jenatzy used an electric-powered car for his daring run in Belgium in 1899. *La Jamais Contente* touched 105.90kph (65.79mph) and became the fastest automobile in the world. He used a streamlined torpedo shape for the car's body. But he did not try to tuck himself and the wheels out of the rush of the wind.

Sunbeam success

In 1927 Britain's Major Henry Segrave broke the 322kph (200mph) barrier in a car with two *Sunbeam* aero-engines. One was in front of the driver and one behind. They were connected together by gears; chains drove the rear wheels. This powerful car took the record at 327.98kph (203.79mph). Segrave's attempt at Daytona Beach in Florida, United States, was the first of many there.

Golden Arrow
With its aircraft engine, Henry Segrave's *Golden Arrow* took the record in Daytona, USA, in 1929 at 372.39kph (231.44mph).

Bluebird
The name *Bluebird* was carried by several cars built by the Campbell family. Sir Malcolm Campbell held the record nine times before his son Donald took over. This, the last of the *Bluebird* cars, was built in 1960. A powerful jet turbine drove all four wheels and enabled Donald Campbell to take the record at 648.28kph (403.10mph) in 1964 at Lake Eyre, Australia.

Rocket power
From 1964 to 1983 only American drivers held the record. One was Gary Gabelich with *The Blue Flame*. This rocket-powered machine actually has four wheels, which the rules now insist on. The front two are side by side. Gabelich averaged 1001.45kph (622.41mph) in 1970 at Bonneville Salt Flats, USA.

Tyreless
Richard Noble drove his car *Thrust 2* to a new record in 1983. A jet engine propelled the 8.2m (27ft) machine over the Black Rock desert in Nevada, United States, at 1019.25kph (633.47mph). It was the first record-breaking car to abandon tyres altogether. Tyres could be torn to pieces by the high speeds, so *Thrust 2* used solid aluminium wheels that skated over the desert surface.

GLOBAL TRAFFIC JAM

Few inventions have had as great an effect on our lives as the motor car. While it has given us the freedom to travel wherever and whenever we want, it has also presented us with serious world-wide problems. We see huge, time-wasting traffic jams all around us. Road accidents kill and injure millions of people every year. And pollution from car exhausts is partly responsible for some of the world's environmental problems, such as acid rain and the "greenhouse effect" - the warming of the Earth's atmosphere. One solution to traffic congestion is the greater use of public transport. To protect the environment we need to make "cleaner" cars that are recyclable and use less petrol, or use alternative sources of power, such as battery or solar power.

Problems and solutions
On the flyover, motorists queue to drive into the big city, bringing with them congestion, fumes and noise. They feel strained and tired before they even reach work. Under the flyover, motorists cruise at normal speed, alongside buses and cyclists who keep safely to the cycle lanes. A balance of different methods of transport helps free the roads and reduce pollution.

City clouds
When sunlight reacts with the gases from car exhausts, the air in big cities becomes thick and foggy. This "smog" sometimes lasts for several days, cutting out sunlight and making it difficult to breathe.

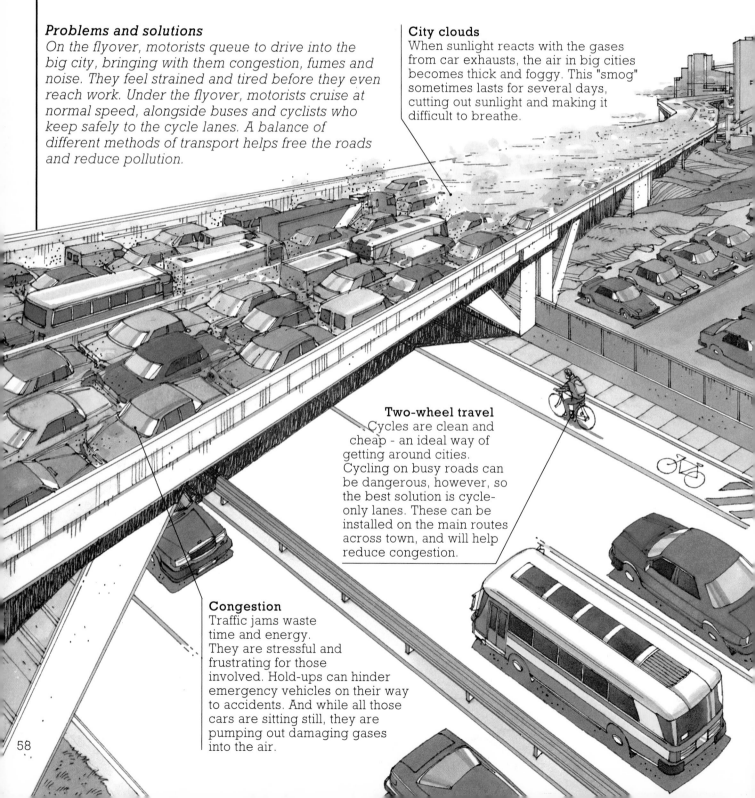

Two-wheel travel
Cycles are clean and cheap - an ideal way of getting around cities. Cycling on busy roads can be dangerous, however, so the best solution is cycle-only lanes. These can be installed on the main routes across town, and will help reduce congestion.

Congestion
Traffic jams waste time and energy. They are stressful and frustrating for those involved. Hold-ups can hinder emergency vehicles on their way to accidents. And while all those cars are sitting still, they are pumping out damaging gases into the air.

Park and ride
Parked cars crowd our city streets. Multi-storey car parks can only meet part of the demand for parking spaces, so some cities now operate "park and ride" systems. People can leave their cars at huge car parks on the outskirts of town, and use free buses that take them to the shops and back.

Forest fate
Gases from car exhausts and factories pollute the atmosphere. When it starts to rain, the rainwater sometimes combines with the pollution and falls as harmful "acid rain". This poisons the waters of inland lakes and rivers, killing fish. It also damages trees. If forests are allowed to die, the animals that live in them will also perish.

Share scheme
Cars often carry only one person. If more people gave each other lifts to work, it would reduce the number of cars on the road. Some cities reserve road lanes and parking areas for cars with at least two passengers.

Clean-up act
Today, most new cars sold in Europe and North America have been fitted with a catalytic converter or "cat". This cleans up some of the poisonous gases from the exhaust. When the exhaust fumes pass through, chemical elements inside the "cat" convert many of these gases to less harmful substances. But it does not remove carbon dioxide. In fact, catalyzed cars use more fuel, and so produce more carbon dioxide. Cars also need to be more fuel-efficient if they are really to be "environment friendly".

Catalyzed engines can only run on unleaded fuel - any lead in the petrol "poisons" the converter and stops it working

A silencer reduces "noise pollution"

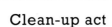

Catalytic converters are most efficient when fitted close to the engine

Better by bus
A bus full of people uses much less fuel than if all its passengers were to drive their own cars. Public transport needs to be cheap and reliable if drivers are to be tempted away from their cars. Many cities have bus lanes, so that buses do not get caught in traffic jams.

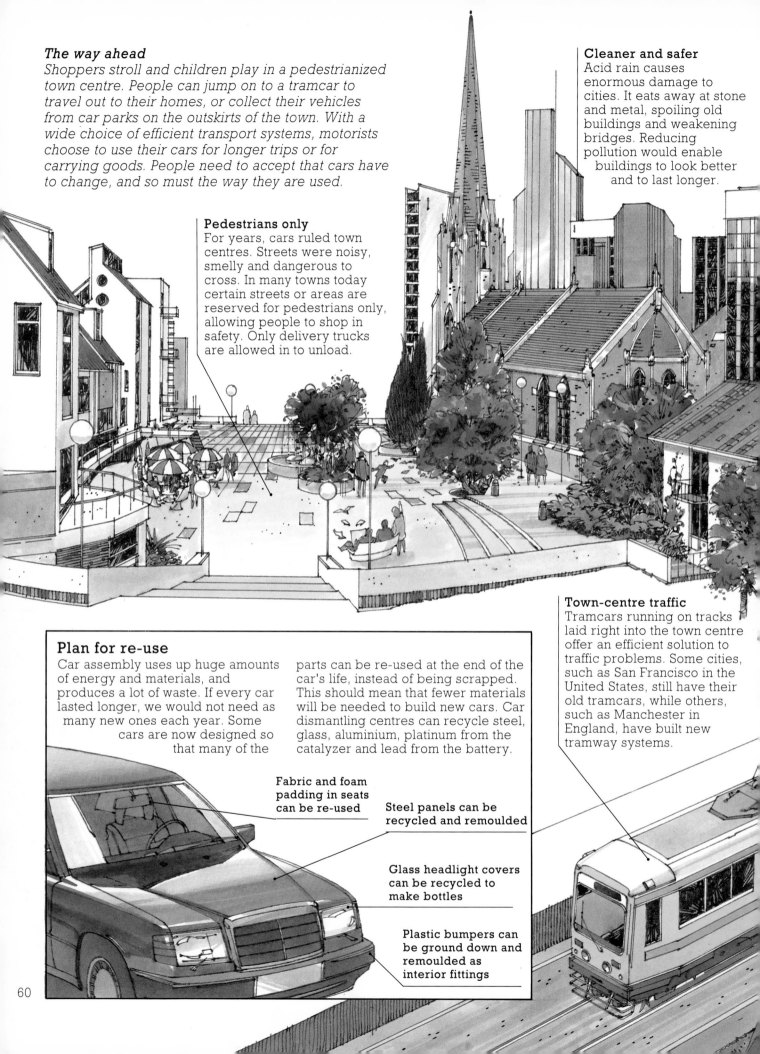

The way ahead
Shoppers stroll and children play in a pedestrianized town centre. People can jump on to a tramcar to travel out to their homes, or collect their vehicles from car parks on the outskirts of the town. With a wide choice of efficient transport systems, motorists choose to use their cars for longer trips or for carrying goods. People need to accept that cars have to change, and so must the way they are used.

Cleaner and safer
Acid rain causes enormous damage to cities. It eats away at stone and metal, spoiling old buildings and weakening bridges. Reducing pollution would enable buildings to look better and to last longer.

Pedestrians only
For years, cars ruled town centres. Streets were noisy, smelly and dangerous to cross. In many towns today certain streets or areas are reserved for pedestrians only, allowing people to shop in safety. Only delivery trucks are allowed in to unload.

Town-centre traffic
Tramcars running on tracks laid right into the town centre offer an efficient solution to traffic problems. Some cities, such as San Francisco in the United States, still have their old tramcars, while others, such as Manchester in England, have built new tramway systems.

Plan for re-use
Car assembly uses up huge amounts of energy and materials, and produces a lot of waste. If every car lasted longer, we would not need as many new ones each year. Some cars are now designed so that many of the parts can be re-used at the end of the car's life, instead of being scrapped. This should mean that fewer materials will be needed to build new cars. Car dismantling centres can recycle steel, glass, aluminium, platinum from the catalyzer and lead from the battery.

Fabric and foam padding in seats can be re-used

Steel panels can be recycled and remoulded

Glass headlight covers can be recycled to make bottles

Plastic bumpers can be ground down and remoulded as interior fittings

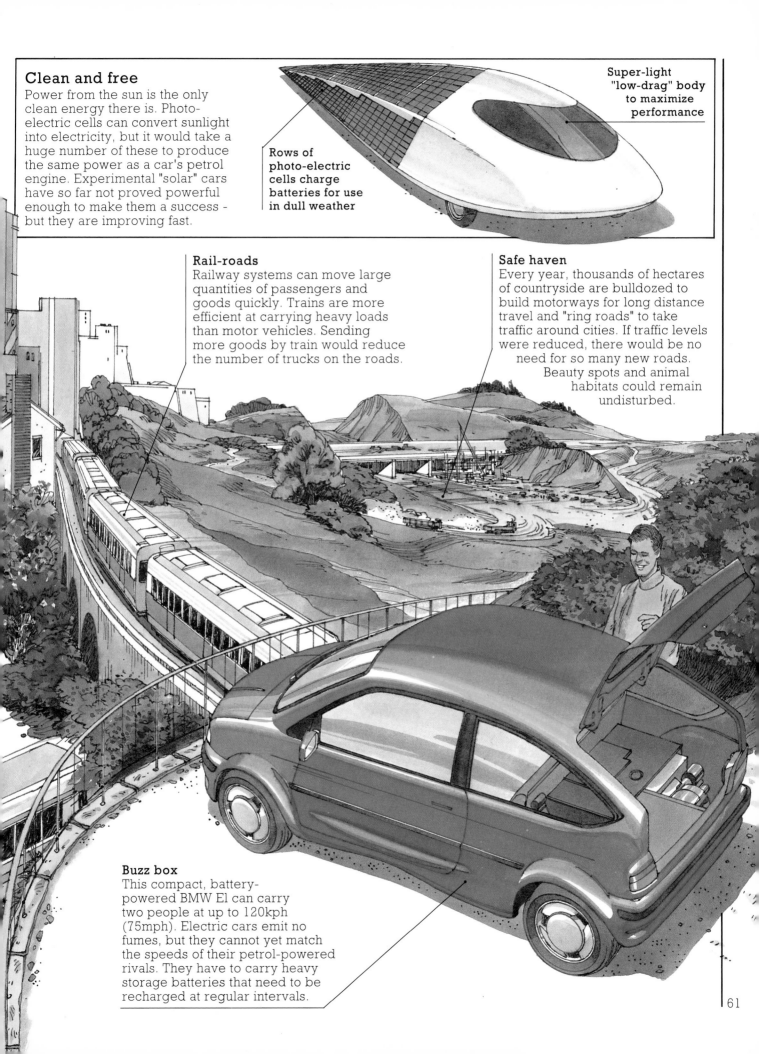

Clean and free

Power from the sun is the only clean energy there is. Photo-electric cells can convert sunlight into electricity, but it would take a huge number of these to produce the same power as a car's petrol engine. Experimental "solar" cars have so far not proved powerful enough to make them a success - but they are improving fast.

Rows of photo-electric cells charge batteries for use in dull weather

Super-light "low-drag" body to maximize performance

Rail-roads

Railway systems can move large quantities of passengers and goods quickly. Trains are more efficient at carrying heavy loads than motor vehicles. Sending more goods by train would reduce the number of trucks on the roads.

Safe haven

Every year, thousands of hectares of countryside are bulldozed to build motorways for long distance travel and "ring roads" to take traffic around cities. If traffic levels were reduced, there would be no need for so many new roads. Beauty spots and animal habitats could remain undisturbed.

Buzz box

This compact, battery-powered BMW El can carry two people at up to 120kph (75mph). Electric cars emit no fumes, but they cannot yet match the speeds of their petrol-powered rivals. They have to carry heavy storage batteries that need to be recharged at regular intervals.

FUTURE CARS

What will cars be like in 30 years' time? Because of environmental problems, car manufacturers are already concentrating on building less wasteful and longer-lasting cars which can be recycled. Scientists are working to produce more efficient batteries, and engines that are powered by hydrogen, gas or alcohol, rather than petrol. Every year at the major motor shows designers unveil their new "concept cars", containing the latest developments in car technology. These one-off creations are the most expensive cars in the world. Each takes several years to create. They not only look extraordinary, but some can also "think" for themselves. Computers control rear-wheel steering, four-wheel drive, navigation and radar. Some of the ideas and gadgetry may appear in next year's family cars, while others may need further improvement before they are widely used.

The way forward

Is this a vision of the future? With their aircraft-style cockpit interiors, electronic push-button controls and dramatic-looking bodywork in bold colours, these concept cars give an impression of what a car of the future could look like. Few are ever built for public sale, but they demonstrate spectacularly the ideas coming out of the designers' studios.

Laser look-out

Many accidents are the result of drivers travelling too close to the car in front. Tomorrow's cars may have laser or radar range-finders to check the distance to the car ahead. When the car is too close, the screen flashes a warning. If the driver ignores it, the system slows the car by closing the throttle or braking.

Under the thumb

Electronic controls, gears, and power steering will alter greatly the interiors of future cars. Buttons on this steering yoke control lights, signals, gear changes, the navigation system and a telephone. They are operated by the thumbs, enabling the driver to keep both hands on the "wheel".

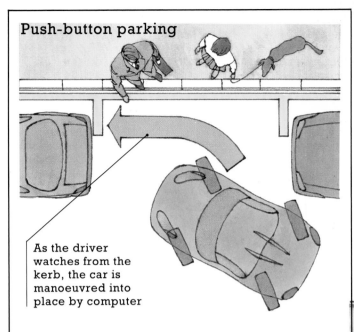

Push-button parking

As the driver watches from the kerb, the car is manoeuvred into place by computer

Here is one answer to the problem of parking in crowded streets. This experimental car parks itself automatically. Its laser and sonic sensors measure up the space around it. A computer guides it into place, using throttle, brakes, automatic gearbox and four-wheel electric steering. The computer even remembers to put the handbrake on!

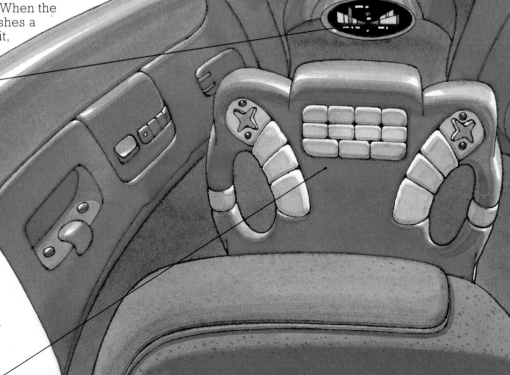

Waterproof weekender
Japan's Mitsubishi RVR was designed as a fun weekend car. It has no roof, no window glass, and no proper doors. The interior is fully waterproofed, including the instruments. Instead of a rear mirror, there is a video camera and a viewing screen on the dashboard.

German ingenuity
Volkswagen's Chico uses two power units. At low speeds it runs on batteries. To accelerate, and at speeds of more than 60kph (37mph), its two-cylinder petrol engine cuts in. The petrol engine also recharges the batteries.

French flair
The sleek Renault Laguna has a carbon-fibre chassis and a turbocharged engine capable of 250kph (155mph). In place of a hood, there is a glass cover which slides over the cockpit when the car is parked.

No more maps
Automatic navigation systems will soon help drivers find their way. An electronic map on a compact disc is displayed on a small screen. Roadside transmitters tell the car where it is, and the car's computer flashes up route instructions. The screen also warns of traffic problems ahead.

Bold and bright
The cockpit of this concept car looks like something out of a science fiction movie. Instead of the traditional instrument panel, sweeping plastic curves enclose a variety of electronic controls and screens. The colourful computer displays enable the driver to see, at a glance, the state of all the car's vital systems.

INDEX

Acknowledgements
Dorling Kindersley would like to thank Janet Abbott, Lynn Bresler, Stephen Commiskey, Dorian Spencer Davis, Jonathan Day, David Humphreys, The Automobile Association, BMW (GB) Ltd, Ford Motor Co., Mercedes-Benz (UK) Ltd, Mitsubishi Motors, the National Motor Museum at Beaulieu, Nissan (UK) Ltd, Vauxhall Motors Ltd, VAG (UK) Ltd, for their help in producing this book.